KW-050-809

Epistles of Inclusion
ST. PAUL'S INSPIRED ATTITUDES

by

W. Graham Monteith

Grosvenor House
Publishing Limited

All rights reserved
Copyright © W. Graham Monteith, 2010

W. Graham Monteith is hereby identified as author of this
work in accordance with Section 77 of the Copyright, Designs
and Patents Act 1988

The book cover picture is copyright to W. Graham Monteith

This book is published by
Grosvenor House Publishing Ltd
28-30 High Street, Guildford, Surrey, GU1 3HY.
www.grosvenorhousepublishing.co.uk

This book is sold subject to the conditions that it shall not, by way of
trade or otherwise, be lent, resold, hired out or otherwise circulated
without the author's or publisher's prior consent in any form of binding or
cover other than that in which it is published and
without a similar condition including this condition being imposed
on the subsequent purchaser.

A CIP record for this book
is available from the British Library

ISBN 978-1-907652-69-1

For my Son, Peter

Contents

Acknowledgements

I should like to thank a number of people for their help with this book, which may not reflect their views. The following people offered help and hints with certain topics: my writing seemed to take off after meeting with members of the *Ecumenical Disability Advocates Network* (EDAN). Kathryn Galloway made some remarks about St Paul which suggested to me that I was on the right track. I twice needed help with topics and Professor John Swinton and Dr Iain A Whyte came to my rescue. Professor Frances Young taught me a lot when I was in Switzerland with EDAN and readily supplied unpublished material some of which is referenced in this book.

I should like to thank the members of *Prospects for Scotland* whom my wife and I met at their annual national gathering in Dunfermline. Branches from all over Scotland came together. Likewise, I owe a warm word of thanks to the Perth Branch of *Faith and Light*, an offshoot of *L'Arche*.

My main help came from the family. For the second time, I have to thank my mother-in-law, Jean Little, for typing most of the book to my dictation. Keeping it in the family, my cousin, Thea Laurie edited the second draft making valuable suggestions and tidying up many of the mistakes I had missed in the previous draft. She was aided and abetted by her husband, John.

I hope that I shall be forgiven for any omissions of expressions of gratitude.

... ...

Biblical quotations are from the *New International Version* (NIV) – International Bible Society, Copyright © 1973, 1978, 1984 by International Bible Society. They have been drawn from *Pradis* CD-ROM – Copyright © The Zondervan Corporation, 2002.

Preface

I have spent much of my life belittling the work of St Paul. His teaching was a small reflection of his Lord, Jesus Christ. However, in the course of writing this book I have had the opportunity to study him in depth and to realise that he had many experiences and ideas which are relevant today as we seek to understand social inclusion.

Originally the title, *Epistles of Inclusion*, was going to end in a question mark because I was so uncertain as to whether Paul had anything positive to say. The question mark is no longer there but it could equally apply to whether we in the Church understand the social inclusion of disabled people or have the will to implement with equality as our goal.

I fear that I may have been unduly harsh on certain writers and attitudes which circulate in the Church. It is difficult for someone with a physical disability to write objectively about people with learning difficulties and their carers. If I have succeeded – I am glad; if I have failed – it is because I am over-zealous in maintaining the independence of disabled people.

Edinburgh

February, 2006

Introduction

Pauline Tradition and Disability

A Professor of New Testament Studies suggested to my divinity class of '72, and probably to all of his students, that after we had been preaching for a few years, we should pile up our sermons into three bundles; Old Testament, Gospels and Epistles. If we discovered that one pile was much higher than the others were, we should review their method of preaching. Sadly, most preachers have preferences and foibles which will probably ensure that one pile is much higher than the rest. The pile of sermons about the gospels would be the tallest in my study, if I had bothered to keep them. This book is about the Epistles and their influence on the churches', and sometimes society's thoughts about disabled people. It is not a study of Pauline and related theology nor is it a study of disability. The discourse of the theology in question here may be divided into two main types: the exegesis of the Epistles and, second, the influence certain doctrines have had on social policy and thinking which has affected disabled people. Such is the subject matter of this book. It will examine the traditions behind the preaching of the epistles and the influence of major historical trends in church history.

When it comes to social inclusion and disability, there is little wonder that the pile of sermons from the Gospels is probably higher. The healing miracles provide vivid illustrations of how Jesus treated and loved people with disabilities. These stories can pluck the heartstrings and inspire sentimental compassion which is often unwarranted. Saint Paul, by contrast, is theological and theoretical in his approach with little sentiment to inspire us. Yet, Paul wrestled with his own disability and sought to include many 'outsiders' in the blessings of his newfound faith. He offered us models of inclusion which only work with the love that Jesus displayed in the more iconic Gospels.

First, to return to the Professor, there are more than personal prejudices involved in the choice of subject matter for sermons which are far more important than a flippant aside during a lecture. St Paul is to many the first Christian theologian and some of his epistles, such as Romans, are justifiably revered for their theological content which gave body to the teaching of Jesus and the growing following which he had after his resurrection and the energising of the apostles by the events of Pentecost. His message remained difficult for large sections of the community and whilst his brother James and others continued to preach of the Jews, Paul developed a specific ministry to the gentiles. They were not more intellectual than the Jews but probably had a completely different and more cosmopolitan way of thinking which Paul was able to tap into and develop in the communities which he visited and to whom he wrote. The world was a small place by our standards at that time but Paul managed to cover much of the known world in his travels which are recorded in the Acts of the Apostles. It is this intellectual content of the existing epistles which makes him so attractive to many theologians and preachers but it masks a truth which is often overlooked.

Paul fought tirelessly to reduce the barriers to groups seeking entry into the young church and we can now imagine how he might have approached the obstacles which people with disabilities have when they yearn for full participation in the church of today.

There are many good reasons why disabled people should not be at the top of preacher's agenda. Whilst it is a tremendously important issue, sermons must address a great many biblical topics and people's concerns with daily living. Disabled people feature in almost every part of the Bible: in the prescriptions of the law, in humorous remarks about the preparedness of armies, in passages of encouragement and of major debate such as in Job, and, of course, in the healing miracles of both the Old and the New Testament. Most of these miracles in the New Testament appear in the Gospels but they do occur less frequently in the Letters of St Paul.

One of Paul's main aims in writing his letters was to encourage unity within the small congregations in his charge and to show them ways of overcoming the social barriers which prevented different classes of people from talking sensibly to each other about the new found faith in Jesus. Paul offered advice and solutions which united Jew and Gentile, woman and man in the same faith and by implication that same advice speaks to us today of the need of include disabled people in every aspect of the church's life and work.

At first sight, the gospels appear to be simple narratives about the life and times of Jesus, about his death and the injustice of it and his resurrection. However, the gospels without exception are theological in the same way as the epistles but with more narrative content. The writers selected the most important aspects of his life and edited his most important teaching to produce a compelling and interesting life story. The reformers who began to offer such a bias towards St Paul in formulating their theology did not forget these facts, which have so often been overlooked. John Knox turned to the Gospel of St John on his deathbed and had Chapter 17, the great prayer of Jesus read aloud to him that had been 'his anchor' for many years. (Graham, 2001; 326) The prayer that can be read as a narrative remains one of the most compelling theological passages in the New Testament. Chapter 17 provides a warrant, albeit historically spurious, in a Gospel for Paul's emphasis on unity. The fact that his writing is such a fruitful foundation for intellectual development has meant that in many reformed churches his thought has been discussed significantly more than the gospels which have appealed to traditions, such as Roman Catholicism, which have theologies that depend on picture stories of Jesus. Both types of documents were aimed at a public audience. For instance, Doty has analysed the Pauline epistles in the light of Hellenic styles of letter writing and argues cogently that Paul's letters were not only testamentary in style, but were open to entire communities. (Doty, 1983) They possessed an authority that reached far beyond any individual recipient to the heart of the fledgling Christian community that received them.

The various ecclesiastical traditions have reflected the desire to control the choice of subjects for sermons by producing lectionaries to guide congregations and pastors in their weekly study of the Bible. Traditionally, reformed churches in the UK and America have shied away from lectionaries believing that it is up to the conscience of the minister to choose the subject matter of his sermon. The Anglican and Roman Catholic traditions have chosen to proscribe appropriate readings for each Sunday that are guided firstly by the Christian Year and then by a systematic review of the Bible that attempts to cover all the major themes in what are known as 'the ordinary Sundays'. The Catholic Breviary is based upon a three year cycle which concentrates on one synoptic Gospel (Matthew, Mark and Luke) whilst John's Gospel is covered during the religious festivals. On the ordinary Sundays in both traditions, the lectionaries are accompanied by a strong guide as to whether to preach from the Gospel reading or the exceptional passage from an epistle or Old Testament. Such devices begin to suggest how the preacher can balance out his piles of sermons.

Certain obvious church traditions have increased the importance of the epistles. Two examples are St. Paul's institution of the Lord's Supper and his description of the Body of Christ which has justifiably become the model for the church community. Each of these will be dealt with in later chapters but should be noticed as obvious examples of Paul's claim to permanence in the churches' thinking. Doctrines which have been developed at various times have an equal importance: considerable space will be devoted to the historical influence of predestination on both the churches thought about disabled people and that of society as a whole and we shall venture outside theology altogether to consider the effect that the 'Protestant work ethic' has had on how people view and consider disabled people.

Academic books about disabled people have a pedantic penchant for explaining models of disability at length and with great justification from contemporary literature. This may well be necessary when we are dealing with matters of health and impairments which affect people's function within society. However, this book is about social inclusion and includes all people who are excluded because of illness or any kind of impairment that prevents them from taking part in a society which puts up physical or psychological barriers. Disabled people are often lonely and isolated from friends who do not have the time to understand the demands of being close to disability or illness. Disabled people often are excluded by the prejudice of employers and social groups alike and feel that the barriers that they must overcome are overwhelming. It is widely thought that people with disabilities often make up rationales to explain their lot in society but this can often be overstressed by an uninformed and concerned public. The fact is that you are more likely to be poor if you are disabled and less likely to be in employment, have a large disposable income or the ability to use transport spontaneously to allow the lifestyle which most take for granted.

Governments in the UK have set up 'social inclusion units' to combat and overcome such isolation and real evidence of their good intention can be found in the strenuous efforts which are now made to give employment opportunities to people with disabilities in public and government appointments. Yet, however much of a favourable gloss one puts on it, disabled people remain isolated, lonely and cut off from many of the mainstream activities that we all take for granted. Faced with such problems it is little wonder that many writers, this one included, take refuge in models and clinical language that sanitizes the loneliness which comes from social exclusion.

Most references to social inclusion in church literature refer to the simple issues of loneliness and isolation. However, government policy is not confined to providing positive discrimination in job interviews and the likes but is seen by many commentators as a much less benign policy in that it is aimed at bringing people off benefits and achieving their social inclusion by offering employment schemes such as the 'New Deal'. It is a policy aimed at not only disabled people but also all kinds of groups from ethnic minorities to single parents. It is widely rumoured that Tony Blair regards many of those excluded as 'benefit junkies' and the entire policy raises questions about whether the search for inclusion is always a positive pursuit by either the government or the church. The simplicity of the churches' model of exclusion is vastly different from the political agenda and it is impossible to ignore the very positive encouragement of the church against a background of controversial policies in both the UK and the USA.

At various points in the book, it will be necessary to consider the medical model of disability and the social model of disability but these will be avoided as much as possible. An American writer, Olkin (1999) uses what she calls the 'minority model' almost synonymously with the social model of disability but avoids the straightjacket of the latter which can be rather cruel in its treatment of social exclusion. Eisland also uses this model in a more political way. In the third chapter of *The Disabled God* (1994), she develops an overview of disabled people's political consciousness as a minority with a voice to raise against the injustices which disabled people face.

Loneliness and isolation cannot, and perhaps should not, be modelled. We will be examining a new compilation of the writings of Stanley Hauerwas who observed the loneliness of people with learning difficulties in institutions in Texas several decades ago. St Paul compels us to look at issues such as isolation because by implication he insists that we are all part of the body of Christ and it is impossible to read these passages in Corinthians without considering those who are excluded.

St Paul did not in fact address issues associated with disabilities and illness. Jesus modelled his ministry around such concerns and so the issue became one of legitimate enquiry by theologians and disabled theorists alike. Paul had however an awareness of illness insofar as he suffered from a 'thorn in his flesh' and experienced temporary blindness and dependency after his conversion on the road to Damascus. He was involved with the miraculous in several ways but these were confined to his history and to his community. The release from prison is an example of a 'historical' miracle which became part of his life history whereas any healings reflected more a concern for the community in which he lived. These matters will be dealt with in the next chapter.

At an earlier point, it was suggested that Paul offered a much more intellectual approach to Christianity than its founder. Within the epistles, models are constructed which can be applied to our treatment of disabled people. The Body of Christ provides one such model for understanding obligations to disabled people and appropriate ways of treating them. This also applies to our understanding of the Lord's Supper or Eucharist and authors like Joel Shuman (2003) offer a response to these themes which compel him to find a model for the treatment of those who are ill implied in our whole understanding and participation in the Eucharist. Paul is unique in the whole of the Bible in offering us the challenge of rich models which can be applied in so many situations. For the sake of correctness, it should be stressed that these models are not exclusively designed to address people with disabilities.

The Epistles of St Paul have given us not only the models just mentioned but also constructs which have been inferred both with theologians and by a society which used to be greatly influenced by religious ideas. One such secondary construct has come out of Paul's ideas of predestination. It can and will be argued that there is an inclusive equality within this doctrine which can potentially motivate congregations to include disabled people but there is a considerable literature which suggests that church people have looked for signs that a person was saved by the quality of his or her life. Although they would wish to deny works have anything to do with salvation, works nevertheless have been seen as signs of upright and worthy lives which might well be more likely to be saved than other less worthy lives. This has put a considerable question mark over disabled people in earlier centuries and even the early decades of this century. Such a construct is not the fault of St Paul but has developed out of an over zealous reading of his theology.

Similarly, the churches have tended to intellectualize the Eucharist to such an extent that Protestant churches in particular have been reluctant to admit people with limited understanding to the Table of the Lord. The fact that Paul's conversion is held up as the model of the first Christian conversion and the prototype of all subsequent conversions has made it difficult to admit that people with learning difficulties have the potential to be converted and to enter knowingly into the fellowship of Christ. Many authors argue that Paul has a very strict and narrow view of human nature but much of this is what we have projected on to Paul by constructing very strict criteria for not only conversion, but also lifestyle and religious initiation. These issues will come up at various points in the book and will suggest that the church has not been as inclusive as Paul might have wished had he lived in our culture.

There are certainly many ways of founding a study of the Acts of the Apostles and the Letters of Paul and others but they probably can be sorted into three basic kinds of analysis that influence the outcome of studies which are based upon them.

First, there is a general acknowledgement by all that the Acts of the Apostles which was written by Luke is really a continuation of Luke's Gospel. After the crucifixion and resurrection of Jesus, Luke's narrative naturally turns to the events of Pentecost and the Ascension of Christ seven days later. It is in a sense a seamless narrative which then documents the expansion of the early Christian community inspired and fortified by the spirit of Pentecost and a growing awareness that the powers which Jesus had and so often tried to pass to his disciples were in fact real and could be enacted in his name as for instance when Peter and James healed a lame beggar at the Golden Gate. This particular story is often used as the launch pad for the theory which undergirds many accounts of these Books of the New Testament because it shows graphically that the healing was done in and through Christ. This story was dealt with at length in an earlier book by Monteith (2005) suggesting that whilst such an interpretation was correct there was always a great temptation to forget the disabled man at the centre of it. This first interpretation of the second half of the New Testament finds testimony to the power of Jesus in the conversion of Paul and his travels which involved many instances of danger from natural events like sea storms or imprisonment by authorities opposed his preaching. Paul himself did not possess supernatural powers nor was his ministry to glorify God in the way in which, it is argued, the miracles of Jesus did but to testify to and glorify Christ crucified and risen. In short, the books which deal with Paul and all the other epistles continue the *kerygma* of the gospels and are part of a unity which is the New Testament.

The second basis for analysing these works moves radically from such a position. It is argued that behind the gospels it is possible to discover the historical Jesus when the text of the narrative are stripped bear of redactions and other devices which are used to gradually develop the *myth* of Jesus Christ. The works of Paul are regarded as theological reflections on a man whom Paul probably never met and upon witnesses who spoke to Paul but are seldom accurately quoted. Jesus without Paul would have been a religious figure without many doctrines or beliefs beyond his crucifixion and the reports of his resurrection. Paul was the first theologian to begin to explain to an audience beyond the radical communities of Israel and, in particular Nazareth, who found within the life of Jesus an eschatological understanding of the last days and found the scriptures of the Old Testament fulfilled in the life of their Saviour Jesus. Paul took it upon himself to expand the understanding of Jesus to communities and indeed a world which looked far beyond radical Judaism. Indeed, a large block of the Acts of the Apostles is taken up with the events leading to the first Christian council which was held in Jerusalem between Jewish Christians, represented by James, and a growing body of Gentile Christians represented by Paul. This explanation has as many attractions as the last one but has also many drawbacks. This analysis represents a forensic examination of how Christianity grew - and grew away from the simplicity which must have been the life of Jesus into the complexity of Christian theology in the first few centuries and beyond. It is tempting to glamorize the simplicity of Jesus' life but it certainly was not as complicated as Paul and all subsequent theologians have made it, yet without such complexity people might not have been inspired to follow such a Saviour and to find within the *myth* so many ways in which their lives could be enriched and guided by many doctrines which gradually unfolded during the life of St Paul and brought comfort and understanding to many.

The third mode of analysis is the one which is most likely to be used here and does not contradict the previous two modes but certainly offers an approach which helps us to understand the nature of the Christian community with all its diversity but also its common foundation. An interesting book written from a Jewish perspective by Alan Segal (1990) has suggested that the key to understanding Paul is to treat him as a convert to a new and exciting community of believers. Paul had a strong conviction that he was living amongst a new and rich community of believers who had previously not been saved by any religious belief or understanding. As Luke describes Paul's conversion of the road of Damascus, he does so in a highly stylised way which is reminiscent of the call of Jeremiah who was called to go from one community to another which was regarded as inferior and less worthy of the Jewish cult. Paul, as in the case of so many Old Testament prophets was struck down by his vision of God speaking through Jesus and was so affected by the power of this experience that he moved from his Pharisaical background and closed community to another which would embrace a variety of people who were previously beyond the knowledge of a strict Pharisee. As Paul was converted, so he believed that all his community must be likewise. The unity of Christians became of priority because the power of conversion could not be shown without a demonstration of the cohesiveness of the community they had joined. For many the phrase, 'Look how these Christians love one another', remained a testimony to the qualities of the new community and underlined the urgency in Paul's writing when he addressed the disunity within the diverse groups of Christians for whom he assumed oversight. This model and the psychology behind it has been owned by the church ever since and can make social inclusion so vitally important to a Church keen to exhibit its vitality in the lifestyle both its members and its organisations adopt. This third way of looking at the works of Paul is therefore vital to the analysis of this book.

Notwithstanding Segal's analysis of faith as being central to Paul's understanding of it as a vitally important characteristic of the burgeoning Christian community, Postliberals like Lindbeck in *The Nature of Doctrine* (1984) and later Harink in *Paul among the Postliberals* (2003) suggest that a new understanding of justification by faith needs a new interpretation to bridge the ecumenical divide. It may also be that their arguments, which will be dealt with in Chapter 6, may well make this difficult doctrine more accessible to people with disabilities. The Enlightenment led to a great emphasis on the 'rational man' – certainly not the 'disabled man' (*sic*) – and perhaps postmodernity has opened a fresh chink of light for others such as disabled people to find acceptance. Commenting on the old order of modernity, Thomas Guarino observes:

> The Enlightenment's concern with methodology as the path to truth caused it to veil historicity and to ignore the nuances, complexities, and ambiguities of being and knowing. This truncated notion of humanity led, in science, to an excessive Baconism that ignored the historical-hermeneutical elements of thought and inappropriately canonized the foundationalisms of positivism and empiricism. Particular postmodern invective is reserved for this kind of rationalism that deified algorithmic positivism, leading ineluctably to technocracy and even totalitarianism.

(Guarino, 1996)

One of the cumulative effects of searching for the 'perfect community' has been the search for unity both within the church communities and within the Church Universal. Many ecumenical documents and organisations have taken their titles or motifs from John's Gospel chapter 17, verse 11 which is most commonly quoted in the authorised version, '... that they may be one [as we are].' Often Latin is appropriate or grander, '*Ut unum sint*'. The high expectations which Jesus prayed for in his disciples continues in the modern mind into the perfect body of Christ and demands a unity which is always going to be idealistic to the point of being unattainable. Texts about the body of Christ are quoted repeatedly as illustrations of where the Church both succeeds and fails. In recent years, the diversity of the human condition has grown as we have become aware of minorities of race, gender, sexual orientation and disability. The famous text from Galatians now bears a burden far beyond the imaginings of St Paul:

> There is neither Jew nor Greek, slave nor free, male nor female, for you are all one in Christ Jesus. (Galatians 3:28)

The modern reader has understood this text to mean that the Body of Christ must be open to all and that no characteristic or status of our human condition can disqualify us from membership. Paul with his rabbinical background probably had certain mystical views about the nature of faith which was available to all but did not actually alter your status. It is more than likely that we have taken the meaning of this text more literally and assume that status does not matter at all. In similar manner, we read the letters to the Corinthians as if they are a direct prescription to us whereas Paul in fact was dealing with very real quarrels and disharmonies within the Church at Corinth, for example, which have often been replicated in the modern church but are not identical. Paul is not solving every problem which faces the defective community which is our church but we can read his letters as clearly pointing towards the ideal.

> I appeal to you, brothers, in the name of our Lord Jesus Christ, that all of you agree with one another so that there may be no divisions among you and that you may be perfectly united in mind and thought. (1 Corinthians 1:10)

A congregation today must decide whether St Paul's appeal is as meaningful to them as it was to the original recipients of the letter and how they can find unity in their own divisions. In the case of disability, it probably has been the case for a long number of years that the exclusion of disabled people has not been an issue and is now becoming one simply because a pressure group is pressing for socially inclusive churches which will not exclude minority groups. It is difficult in the case of Paul to understand that he did not have to address the divisions that we now have in our society yet would have, had they existed within his mindset. Paul was not concerned about disabled people in the way our generation is, nor was he concerned to integrate gays or races which he never knew existed into his church, but we have added on expectations which arise directly from our concern for unity in our society.

These expectations are part of the subject matter of this book as they relate of disabled people and three types of subject matter must be reviewed to help us classify these expectations. First, literature about the nature of gifts will have to be considered because for too long people with disabilities have had their gifts overlooked. Second, the professions and the churches have successfully isolated people with disabilities in ways which are no longer acceptable and if church is truly the Body of Christ, there must be a new impetus to overcome the temptation of isolation with an expanded understanding and concern. Third, the l'Arche community amongst others has shown how the qualities of unity can be built into a church which accommodates disabled people as equals.

John Swinton (2004) has produced a book that compiles much of Stanley Hauerwas' understanding of the theology of disability in an accessible way which has not been available since 1988. It combines a comprehensive collection of his work with commentaries or dialogues by other experts in the field in an interesting and readable format and dismisses pessimistic and defeatist attitudes which have in the past condemned 'the retarded' to institutionalized lives. The result is a fascinating journey through the ethics of writing about and for people with learning difficulties ('the retarded'). It questions how we should best offer them dignity and a place in our midst.

Much of what Hauerwas writes is aimed at parents and addresses the problems of bringing up children with such difficulties.

Stanley Hauerwas raises questions about personhood and the nature of care. He challenges the Churches to accept the 'mentally handicapped' and to understand the true meaning of 'weakness' in the way Christians should accept society's most vulnerable into a community that displays values which are more compassionate and inclusive than society as a whole. A number of friendly critics raise issues around the ethics of writing about disability and challenge Hauerwas to develop an understanding of what it means to give disabled people independence in community homes and the opportunity to develop their own identities.

It is necessary to concentrate upon people with learning difficulties because St Paul has so intellectualized that history has found it very easy to marginalize such people. Swinton's own field is mental health and once again we will see that this shows up a new set of problems. It is wrong, however, to consider that Pauline theology and its social traditions only affect those with a mental disability. Sam Kabue (Fritzson and Kabue, 2004) chooses texts from St Paul to show how he overcame his disability of blindness and it is right and proper to consider whether these texts are properly and usefully applied when they refer to Paul's own affliction which will be dealt with in chapter one.

Next, the interlinked topics of the Body of Christ and the Eucharist will be raised at various points as it relates to society's tendency to label and isolate people. Joel Shuman in *The Body of Compassion* (2000) argues that to treat the individual in terms of medicine or bioethics as an isolated subject or individual is to forget that humanity is potentially united as one in the Body of Christ. In this argument, he is not alone and it will make an interesting topic in the context of this book.

Last, the development of the l'Arche offers material which is rich in the original Roman Catholic traditions of Jean Vanier from Canada who turned from academia to care for, at the outset, two men with learning difficulties in 1964. It has grown into an international movement and is now non-denominational or is even open to secular interpretation. Vanier's primary concern was with the brokenness of many bodies who are victims of injustice of their disabilities, inner city violence or drugs. The word 'brokenness' is now slightly contentious but does not undermine the search of l'Arche for the ideal community of the weak and vulnerable. Frances Young, an academic theologian from Birmingham, has devoted much time to explaining her own relationship and that of society to her profoundly disabled son and has offered many reflections on the meaning of l'Arche.

The literature so far mentioned deals mainly with the constructs which are directly derived from the theology of Paul but when it comes to considering the constructs which society has made and broadly based upon Pauline traditions there is only one author who inspires all others, that is, Max Weber. In particular, there can be no analysis of the effect of the Reformation on disabled people without relating it to Weber's *Protestant Ethic and the Spirit of Capitalism*. (1958) Practically everything that has been written on the effect of the Reformation as a sociological movement has to acknowledge some debt to this work.

Plan of Book

It remains in this introduction to describe the following chapters. The principle interest is in the traditions that have built up around the hermeneutics of St Paul and how this has impinged on the lives of people with disabilities. No chapter attempts to present a comprehensive overview of Pauline theology but develops the type of arguments that have followed from the churches' understanding of Paul and of disability as it has been informed by Pauline theology. It will sometimes be difficult to distinguish between illness and disability.

This book is divided into three parts that each offer different insights into the nature and shortcomings of inclusion. In Parts

Two and Three, the first chapter of each section examines the intentions of Paul, whilst the others outlines some of the modern consequences.

Chapter One is the only chapter that is really concerned with the biographical facts of Paul. Paul encounters illness or disability twice in his life. Throughout his ministry he suffered from a 'thorn in his flesh' and from temporary blindness after his conversion. Paul used this thorn to illustrate certain truths about Christian suffering and perseverance that will have to be discussed at length. Many texts surrounding Paul's sufferings have been used to encourage or comfort those with disabilities. Is this justified? Whilst Paul was acquainted with healing and with miraculous events, it must be asked why he did not heal personally on a grander scale nor make it a major feature of his ministry, as did Jesus.

Chapter Two is a bit of a digression but is of some importance. It is a digression because we move from Paul's letters to those with other authorships. Whilst Paul may not have been a notable healer, the letter of James offers much advice on healing that cannot be ignored. The letter to the Hebrews says nothing about disability. Indeed, it may hint that disability is a disqualification to certain religious rites but it offers a tremendous insight into the alienation of Christians at the time and suggest ways in which minority groups should review their Christian convictions today.

Part Two is devoted to the Body of Christ, perhaps Paul's most important doctrine. Chapter Three shows how he built up a spiritual community that was inclusive of all who had been baptized into the new and exciting band of converts to Christianity.

Chapter Four will be devoted to caring visionaries who have developed truly inclusive communities by welcoming people with disabilities into the Body of Christ. Nevertheless, this will be couched in a series of questions about the workings of the Body of Christ.

Chapter Five, the last in this section, deals with the problems of baptism and eucharist that have always been the visible sign of unity amongst Christians. There have been, however, many reasons why disabled people have found it hard to be part of these uniting acts and this chapter will explore reasons why. I draw on my own experience as well as other sources here. Whilst the mass had been open to allebrHebrewsHebrews He who met the simple requirements of the non-reformed churches, Protestant churches tended to stress the importance of self-examination and of conscious reflection prior to partaking at the Lord's Table. What kind of effect did this have on people with disabilities?

Part Three is devoted to issues which arise from the work of the Reformers and of the Reformation. Chapter Six will look at the implications of the doctrines of Predestination and Justification by Faith alone. These doctrines intellectualized Christianity to an extent that had never been present in the Roman Catholic Church. It is not the intellect of the theologians, which will concern us, but the demands that were placed on the every church member. The church before the Reformation had been blessed by intellects of tremendous import but the demand was not placed upon members as it was to be in the centuries following the Reformation. Were disabled people excluded because their lifestyles or intellectual capabilities failed to reflect the general expectations of congregations up and down the lands?

A third component of the Reformation was its heralding of equality and democracy within the structures of the church. Did equality really manifest itself and have people with disabilities ever really benefited?

The final chapter in this part will ask whether 'inclusion' is little more than illusion in contrast to equality.

The conclusion of the book will be that all theology is volatile and dangerous in the wrong hands or when not handled with care. Disabled people have been damaged by some of the traditions, which have come from St Paul, but there are ways of avoiding these and some of these will have been highlighted.

Part One

Healing within the Body

Chapter One

Paul's Experience of Disability

St Paul refers to a 'thorn in the flesh' in the twelfth chapter of 2 Corinthians in a rare autobiographical reference to himself and his trials. The nature of this thorn is open to endless debate and will never be resolved but it is important because people have speculated upon Paul's affliction and have applied it to themselves in many different circumstances. To say that Paul was disabled is facile. Ill he may have been; disabled in the modern sense of the word he certainly was not. Furthermore, like many ageing people today, Paul probably accepted his impairment with stoic resignation that only occasionally bubbled over into frustration as in Corinthians and elsewhere in Galatians.

It is for this reason that we shall cut to the chase and explain how the modern mind might regard him as disabled and thereby apply insights into his life. There are so many constructs of disability that it is probably better to avoid them and consider rather the question of whether his illness would come under the terms of the *Disabled Discrimination Act, 1995* (DDA). It took several years prior to the drafting of this Act to reach a satisfactory definition of disability. Does impairment prevent you from taking part in certain activities? How long does it have to last before it counts as a permanent disability? What about invisible disabilities or mental illness? All these questions were at the back of the minds of the working party who prepared the way for the Act. There can, of course, be arguments about whether the Act has been framed in ways which are acceptable to those who favour a particular model of disability, but our concern is not with the past arguments but whether Paul today would have qualified as a disabled person.

Paul was a tent maker by profession but in common with others of the time, he was able to combine his practical work with study and preaching as a fairly learned Pharisee and subsequently a Christian.

His activities were interrupted on his own testimony by his disability but luckily he did not appear to suffer discrimination but rather the people of Galatia showed considerable goodwill and desire to help him when Paul attests that '... if you could have done so, you would have torn out your eyes and given them to me.' (Galatians 4: 15) This suggests that something was wrong with Paul's eyes but the jury will remain out in this matter a little longer.

The DDA defines disability very simply in the first clause of the Act:

> **1.** - (1) Subject to the provisions of Schedule 1, a person has a disability for the purposes of this Act if he has a physical or mental impairment which has a substantial and long-term adverse effect on his ability to carry out normal day-to-day activities.

> (2) In this Act "disabled person" means a person who has a disability.

The third clause of the Act gives powers to the Secretary of State to produce Schedules that define the precise types of disabilities that should qualify. So, for instance, AIDS is now accepted as a disability under the Act as are many types of mental illness. The complexity of the Act lies, however, in the case law that is built up in the courts and tribunals as the legality of dismissals and exclusions are tested. No such complexity would have existed at the time of St Paul but nowadays he would have been protected by a multitude of regulations, which have been spawned by the Act.

It is difficult, nevertheless, to determine whether Paul's 'thorn in the flesh' was really a disability. Most commentators put forward three possible interpretation of the phrase, 'thorn in my flesh' and each has considerable merit and has entered our vernacular as ways of describing an irritant. First, the phrase is often understood to denote social oppression. Paul was oppressed by recalcitrant groups within the budding church communities or by the Jewish and Roman authorities who both imprisoned him and had him scourged at various times as reported in the Acts of the Apostles by Luke. Paul said that he received this affliction 'from Satan' (2 Corinthians 12:7). This would indicate that he was fighting a righteous war against forces of darkness to bring his new message of faith in Christ Risen to the communities with which he worked. Such a meaning has become very common in secular language. Tony Benn was 'a thorn in the flesh' of the Labour party is but one example. This meaning seems to read more into the text than is there and Paul never asked to be released from the trials of the authorities although he did ask to be released from the pain of his affliction.

Second, many have interpreted it as psychological oppression. The case of Søren Kierkegaard illustrates this well. The father of Christian existentialism used the phrase often to describe his own frame of mind.

> This theme of inner suffering as the source and energy behind Kierkegaard's authorship runs as a *leitmotiv* through the journal entries from their beginning in 1834 to their end in 1855. (Thompson, 1967; p 14)

The idea of 'inner suffering' can be taken a stage further in any analysis of Kierkegaard who had as one of his major themes the development of personality and existence – the coming of the true self. It is only in the maturity of conquering our fears of people and of society that we begin to develop our mature personalities that may be free to serve God. (Hong, 2003; p 114f).

Yet another more plausible explanation of social oppression is that Paul found that his opponents criticised his imperfections as a disqualification for any religious office.

> The old Jewish law required the priest to be physically blameless, and Paul was not physically blameless, and the Jewish party cited this fact as an evidence that he was no true priest of God. Truth came to Paul by degrees, as it does to the rest of us, and through hard experience. So at last it dawned upon him that the weaker he

was and the less able by any means of his own to produce great impression, the stronger was the testimony to the power of the truth and the greatness of the divine life of which he was the minister. (Abbott, 1898; p 167)

Paul may have been imperfect in two ways: He certainly regretted, and possibly regarded as sin, that as Saul he persecuted Christians to such an extent. In addition, if he were carrying a physical disability, he would normally be excluded from religious office. Many disabled people feel that they are excluded from office in the Church and society for precisely these reasons, and so may carry a 'thorn in the flesh' with them in the same way as Paul did. If this is too fanciful, let us be reminded that all of us carry regrets from our past life into the present day.

Third, the jury must at last consider whether Paul actually had a physical impairment or illness which caused him great suffering, which he overcame with courage of which he was prepared to speak in his Epistles.

There are three candidates for physical impairments that might have afflicted St Paul but before discussing them, it is probably better to deal with the one known example of disability that we are sure Paul experienced. There are three accounts in the Acts of the Apostles of his conversion on the road to Damascus. A number of the differences are not important to this theme but it is important to distinguish between Luke's reports of what happened to Paul in chapters 9 and 21 of Acts and words, which are reported to be Paul's own, and which reflect upon the experience of blindness in a court of law before the governor, Festus, in chapter 26.

They have in common the story that Paul encountered the voice of Jesus on the road to Damascus and that this was accompanied by a brilliant light, which temporarily incapacitated him and left him blind for a period of three days. The reports differ in that in the first one Paul was directed to Ananias to be healed of his temporary blindness whilst the second account suggests that Ananias was sent to heal Paul despite protestations that Saul's past conduct meant that he was deserving of all the punishment that God could mete out upon him for persecuting Christians so violently. The speech before Festus will be important because it contains an explicit explanation of Paul's own understanding of his blindness during that period. The most important passage is Luke's first version, Acts chapter 9:

> 8 Saul got up from the ground, but when he opened his eyes he could see nothing. So they led him by the hand into Damascus. 9 For three days he was blind, and did not eat or drink anything.
>
> 10 In Damascus there was a disciple named Ananias. The Lord called to him in a vision, "Ananias!"
>
> "Yes, Lord," he answered.
>
> 11 The Lord told him, "Go to the house of Judas on Straight Street and ask for a man from Tarsus named Saul, for he is praying. 12 In a vision he has seen a man named Ananias come and place his hands on him to restore his sight."
>
> 13 "Lord," Ananias answered, "I have heard many reports about this man and all the harm he has done to your saints in Jerusalem.

Luke suggests that when Paul's sight was restored 'scales' fell from his eyes and he saw clearly again. When the word 'thorn' is used, the Greek word suggests precisely that or possibly a stake – something that was sharp and potentially painful. John Hull however does not concentrate on the nature of Paul's blindness but upon the fact that the blindness is either interpreted by him as a living metaphor or as an illustration of what conversion implies. If both of these are combined, Paul presents the image of a man who is deeply troubled by the awareness that the assumptions which we had previously made about life as a Pharisee were now completely false in the light of the revelation of Christ. Blindness is a vehicle through which he can describe the process and experience of conversion and how the metaphor could be continued into other lives as indeed it was in Acts 13 when we have the story of the blindness of Elymas who was punished for his unusual practices as a magician. (See Hull, 2001; p 59ff) Paul's account of his own blindness appears as words from God quoted in his speech to Festus in Acts 26 verse 15 and on:

15 "Then I asked, 'Who are you, Lord?'

"'I am Jesus, whom you are persecuting,' the Lord replied. 16 'Now get up and stand on your feet. I have appeared to you to appoint you as a servant and as a witness of what you have seen of me and what I will show you. 17 I will rescue you from your own people and from the Gentiles. I am sending you to them 18 to open their eyes and turn them from darkness to light, and from the power of Satan to God, so that they may receive forgiveness of sins and a place among those who are sanctified by faith in me.

These words contain many of the common beliefs about blindness. It was often assumed in the Old Testament that people who departed from the word of God or from proper observance of his ways were blind or deaf and restoration meant finding the path to walk with God again. Disabled people have laboured for a long time under the mistaken belief that blindness was the result of sin and here it is reiterated in this speech. There is also a suggestion that whereas the Jews had walked in the light now they walked in darkness unguided by the light that led the new Christians forward. To walk in the darkness, metaphorically or in reality, was in some way satanic or evil compared with the light of those with eyes seeing physically or spiritually. Hull sums up his argument thus:

In a similar way, to be blind was to be under a curse, but a similar paradoxical inversion had brought Paul into the light of a glorious heavenly vision and thrust the objects of his mission into blindness. (Hull, 2001; p 56)

Now, the fact that Paul may have used his temporary blindness to construct a metaphor about the salvation of Christians after conversion does not mean that Paul's blindness was a fabrication.

It is completely probable that Paul found in his blindness an opportunity to show to others the meaning of conversion. There are other places in his letters where he make a virtue of his 'thorn in his flesh' and we should not dismiss the very real possibility that he was struck down on the road to Damascus and was deeply distressed by being dependent upon others and by the pain of his illness. It was also during this episode that he personally experienced healing - Ananias laid his hands upon him and healed him. (Acts 9:17) Later when Paul is recounting the gifts of members of the Body of Christ, he includes healers and this may well be a reference back to his experience. (1 Corinthians 12:9)

Returning to the decision before the jury, it is now possible to suggest the three candidates for Paul's disability:

1. Paul had an unsightly deformity.
2. Paul developed a periodic illness.
3. Paul had, indeed, an impairment of the eyes.

According to the author of *The Acts of Paul*, written in about 160 AD, Paul was not a good-looking man, in fact, his appearance was quite off-putting and he was noted for his ungainly stature, and that was written by an admiring presbyter! (James, 1924) None of that is politically correct but suggests that we must consider whether he had a deformity which caused others distress. Paul maintains that whatever was wrong with him was 'received from the Lord himself' and one journalistic writer, A N Wilson, has suggested that he did in fact meet the Lord as one of the arresting party in the Garden of Gethsemane and that he was the one who lost his ear when Malchus drew his sword. (Wilson, 1992; chapter II) There is also a tradition that Paul was a hunchback, which, of course was a prescribed deformity in Leviticus 17 preventing such people from becoming priests. It is entirely possible that with certain eye infirmities he could have had an awkward appearance that may have been noted when he was reported to have stared intently at an audience. None of these possibilities is really convincing nor do they have much scholarly support. Paul really cannot be blamed for not being good looking.

Paul may have been plagued by a periodic illness which caused him great distress in the way many people are affected by such debilitating factors in their lives. Many people cope with such illnesses and accept that their lives will be disrupted by episodes of ill-health from time to time but for many it is also a frustration too many and may lead to depression and an awareness of the precariousness of life. The starkest modern examples today are HIV/AIDS and ME which saps the body of strength and which has so far denied satisfactory investigation by doctors. In Paul's case the most likely candidate would be malaria which can have a late onset and in days before prophylactic medicine that could delay and relieve the symptoms. This is the likely explanation of the 'thorn', which is favoured by Wilkinson and by a large number of commentators who wrote in the early twentieth and late nineteenth century. All the recorded attacks of illness which Paul experienced are recorded at a time in his career somewhat after his conversion and Luke, as a physician, was obviously interested enough to record them. Paul describes his first attack himself in 1 Corinthians 12:2–8 which took place in Celicia but other attacks are reported in Antioch (1 Corinthians 13:13–14) and there was a third one in Troas which Paul again mentioned in 1 Corinthians 12:8. Wilkinson argues that this illness must not be associated with events surrounding Paul's conversion but there seems to be no logical reason why this should be so. He concludes:

> In the circumstances, no conclusion can be final, but it seems reasonable to conclude that a diagnosis of malaria is in keeping with the features required of the thorn in the flesh as set out in the two passages we have just considered, more than that of any other disease which has been suggested. It also has the advantage of harmonising with the earliest tradition which described headache as the nature of the thorn, for headaches which can be very severe and disabling are a characteristic feature of malaria. (Wilkinson, 1998; p 226)

Wilkinson and others have certainly described something that Paul suffered in his flesh but the word 'thorn', both in English and in

Greek, suggests something that was both painful and a major irritant to both Paul's flesh and mind. Malaria does not take account sufficiently of the acute pain that a thorn might cause. So the search continues.

Paul suffered some complaint associated with the eyes but not with blindness unless it is temporary. It is equally likely that Paul suffered from an inflammation or pain in the eyes that caused a stabbing sensation somewhat like a thorn and irritated them to such an extent that he felt quite debilitated by the experience. Contrary to Wilkinson, there is so reason for not including his conversion experience where we are told that when Ananias cured him 'scales' fell from his eyes. An irritant in the eyes so deep that it caused blindness and something that continued to bother him throughout his career. He dictated most of his letters and when he wrote, he wrote with an outsized hand. When he preached, his eyes pierced his audience as if they attracted attention perhaps because they looked so painful. He was healed by Ananias but we are never told that he was cured. The people of Galatia had such sympathy for him that they would have gladly have offered their eyes to assist him. Such a theory has quite a number of supporters and at the end of the day, they are as entitled to an opinion on this elusive matter as proponents of other theories.

Bruce Chilton presents a diagnosis that is both convincing and comprehensive involving all the elements of previous diagnoses. He not only suggests that Paul's eyes were affected but also squares the circle by relating it to stress and to his episodic blindness at the time of his conversion. (Chilton, 2004) Paul was suffering from herpes zoster otherwise known as shingles. Shingles is a virus which comes from chickenpox and is carried by most adults but only occasionally results in the characteristic rash and blistering which is similar to chickenpox. It tends to attack when people are tired, stressed or shocked and comes with as associated ache or pain around the affected area. There is no limit as to how many times it may attack and if it is around the face, it can affect the mouth or eyes as a sharp irritant that cannot easily be alleviated. If eyes are affected, blindness or blurred vision may follow. Paul was no stranger to stress and according to Chilton one of these attacks followed a stoning at Lystra (Acts 14:19). Chilton is so convincing that this explanation will suffice amongst many possible candidates and the fact that it accommodates other explanations such as mental oppression adds to its attractiveness. (Chilton, 2004, p 126ff)

Chilton uses the baptism of Paul by Ananias to illustrate how healing can be brought about without a cure. Paul arrived at his house seeking a remedy for his pain and distress following his Damascus experience. He found relieve in the emersion of baptism but was not cured as the scales fell away from his eyes at that time. Chilton shows, contrary to Wilkinson, how important it is to link the whole of Paul's life with a thread of suffering running throughout his life. (Chilton 2004, p 60f) We are thus offered an explanation that satisfies two out of the three contenders for explanations of Paul's 'thorn in the flesh'.

It is beyond doubt that Paul suffered anguish and pain from this illness. Unless his eyesight was actually impaired, he could not be considered a disabled person in terms of the DDA. Nevertheless, there is compelling, emotional feeling behind the story to believe that he shared the frustration of a disability with generations before and still to come. Is it possible to learn lessons about Paul's reaction that show how we regard disability today?

Just as Paul was the first convert to Christianity and became a model for most subsequent converts, so Paul was the first Christian to have a notable disability or illness. Theologians throughout the ages have projected the 'Damascus experience' onto the lives of well-known Christians and countless anonymous pilgrims alike. In a similar way to the 'thorn in the flesh', the 'Damascus Road' has entered our vocabulary as a way of describing any sudden change of mind or viewpoint. This is a tribute to the deeply ingrained biblical tradition that exists in western literature. Paul's disability has become a source of inspiration to many and the way it has been used is distinctively different from some of Paul's doctrinal points, such as the Body of Christ, which has caused theologians to infer the implications for disabled people rather than point towards Paul's own life as an example of dealing with suffering.

To reiterate, theologians can meditate on how Paul coped with disability in three ways. There is firstly, the dramatic effect on his eyes by the vision of Christ on the road to Damascus; secondly, there are Paul's own reflections and thirdly, there is the construction of Paul's life as an outstanding example of success in living gracefully with a disability. A general reservation can be made about all of these. When Karl Marx stated that 'religion was the opium of the people', he was stressing that many poor and oppressed people found meaning and comfort in their suffering from their profound faith in God. Yes, he was against religion but at the same time, he had a profound compassion for those who needed faith to give them meaning in their lives. There must be grave reservations about some of the projections people have placed on Paul's 'thorn in the flesh' for precisely this reason. Some of the projections place intolerable burdens upon people with disabilities.

Let us examine firstly, John Hull's understanding of Paul's blindness after his conversion. There is no reason to believe that Hull does not accept that Paul was temporarily blinded but he then seems to suggest that this was turned into some kind of metaphor to illustrate an intellectual crisis in his life. Such crises are common in most people's lives – common but perhaps not as dramatic. Alisdair MacIntyre describes the term 'epistemological crisis' to denote the way individuals formulate their difficulties in coming to terms with a new state of knowledge. They often do so in terms of dramatic narrative and MacIntyre argues that the only study of this is in fact Hamlet. In the play, Hamlet returns to Elsinore and has to come to terms with the death of his father, the new marital status of his mother and the rule of Claudius. He also had to relate to friends who were not familiar with the new ideas of Wittenburg, such as Rosencrantz and Guildenstern. Hamlet's two friends were in all likelihood still Roman Catholics and had not been exposed to the new thinking of the Reformation. Hamlet himself was struggling with his new learning and the struggle emerges in the play. One notable example is when he finds his stepfather at prayer and has the ideal opportunity to kill him but he remembers that someone dying in a state of grace, e.g., either at prayer or having just received absolution after confession, were assumed to avoid eternal damnation. Hamlet did not want his stepfather to die in a state of grace, which was a throwback to his earlier Catholicism. The portrayal of Hamlet is a supreme dramatic example of how a person had to come to terms with a new universe of emotions and ideas in exactly the way that Paul had to realise that his life was changed. Paul was being asked to move to a new and strange community of people with relative untried beliefs and faith leaving behind the certainties of Judaism and of his pharisaic scheme of things. The blindness of the past was washed away by the waters of baptism and he was welcomed with eyes ablaze in the new light of the Christian faith and community.

The temptation to find hidden meaning in a disability is very strong in people who suffer beyond endurance. By turning a whole episode into a metaphor, their life can assume a new meaning. The moment of an accident becomes the moment when a meaningless life becomes meaningful. Consider, for example, Joni Eareckson (Eareckson Tada, 1991) When Joni had her diving accident as a teenager she underwent a dramatic change of life which eventually found peace and reconciliation in her Christian faith of which she has written so strongly ever since. However, to turn the accident into a crisis caused by God and her treatment and endurance into tests sent by God seem to be asking us to believe in a God who achieves inspirational ends by cruel means. This, I believe is neither a sustainable nor fulfilling understanding of the workings of God and when we come to consider disability as a gift a more creative way of understanding this will be put forward.

Furthermore, if Joni's accident was the result of youthful enthusiasm or carelessness is this an excuse for God allowing it to happen? Is this equally true of drunk drivers or negligence by transport operators? If the answer is yes to these questions, the matter of faith becomes even more problematic because people must rationalise why this has happened and so the crisis in their lives grows. The more faith is used as a metaphor, the more difficulties occur in its use as an explanation. Faith as such is not a compensatory gift in the light of a tragic accident, but is rather a tool to be used to create a life that shines beyond the crisis of an accident towards the path, which leads to acceptance of the new situation.

The next contribution that has been adopted by theologians concerns a constellation of ideas surrounding the doctrine of grace. Paul suffered considerably from his 'thorn in the flesh', which we now accept as an irritation of the eyes, yet he was convinced that God's grace was sufficient. To live in a state of grace means that one accepts God's will and purpose and seeks at all times to imitate Jesus Christ to the best of one's ability and means. The reward of living in such a state is a certain comfort, or in the words of the old hymn, 'a blessed assurance'. In 2 Corinthians Paul tackles the issue at the very beginning before referring to any of his own trials.

> Now this is our boast: Our conscience testifies that we have conducted ourselves in the world, and especially in our relations with you, in the holiness and sincerity that are from God. We have done so not according to worldly wisdom but according to God's grace. (2 Corinthians 1:12)

A gracious man or woman shows qualities that we can all recognise of holiness, serenity and a certain unworldly quality which marks them off from others. With grace comes the spirit and all the gifts that are associated with the spirit. Paul believed that if he had these gifts, he could boast of them not because he earned any credit from them but because they were God given. In chapter 12, however, he applies grace to the way in which he copes with his 'thorn in the flesh'. He suggests that the qualities quoted above are not diminished by his disability but are in fact accentuated, especially when he feels so depressed that he would rather be accepted his afflictions were given by the devil and give in to the despair which they might have caused. He asserts nevertheless in 2 Corinthians 12:9 that the Lord had told him that 'My grace is sufficient for you, for my power is made perfect in weakness.' The second part of this verse will be dealt with later, but Paul is absolutely convinced that God will give him the qualities to overcome the 'weakness' in his flesh which so beset him.

Paul's experience is not unique – it is the nature of the church that Paul's experience became an example of good experience to others. To have grace is to overcome disability. Alas, within this last sentence lies the undoing of many people with disabilities. If a disabled person cannot be cured but can accept a degree of healing that healing may depend upon his or her graciousness. Over the years, this sort of belief has fostered an attitude that disabled people possess a goodness that may in fact be a burden which they cannot carry. There is an expectation in the church that disabled people of faith have an extraordinary faith that carries them forward. Most of them feel that their faith is neither stronger nor weaker than that of any other member and that their gracious qualities are no different from anyone else's. When disabled people discuss politically correct language they discourage the glamorisation of their triumphs over disability because they create unrealistic expectations which they cannot live up to. This experience is common to both church and secular life.

The other use of grace is illustrated well by the experience of Samuel Kabue. He was brought up in Kenya and it was expected that his blindness could be treated by faith healers and cured by their miracles. As a boy, he was subjected on more than one occasion to this unrealistic expectation. He was also exposed to the idea that the lack of cure was due to his lack of faith or that of his parents and his inability to take advantage of these healing opportunities was tantamount to wilful sin. In such a situation, he came to understand that grace was not only a way of acceptance but also a compensation in a society which had unrealistic expectations. He writes;-

> ... I am reminded of St Paul the apostle who, though he had performed many miracles ranging from healing to raising the dead,

lived with a problem which he refers to in 2 Corinthians12:7–9 as a thorn in the flesh. He testified that he pleaded with God about this three times, but God's answer to him was "My grace is sufficient for you." My understanding of this is that our physical conditions should never be grounds to make us not carry out the mission God appoints us to fulfil. God will accompany us and give us the necessary grace to handle all the situations we encounter. (Fritzson and Kabue, 2004; p 40)

Whilst grace may be a burden of some disabled people others find it a creative opportunity as did Paul. When grace represents a counter-sign within society it is indeed creative. Samuel Kabue's society expected miraculous cures and believed that God's power would take away these differences which caused so many problems. In the same way, Paul must have been aware that his communities remained uncomfortable when confronted with his illness. However, in both cases, the fact that they were living by grace meant that their disabilities became subservient to the ministry they had received from God. If such a fact is accepted without fuss and without high expectations being placed on them, there is a very real creative opportunity for something good to be brought about in their circles.

The last issue that Paul understands surrounding his 'thorn in the flesh' involves the second part of the verse quoted above. It bears quoting again:

"My grace is sufficient for you, for my power is made perfect in weakness.".

The second clause of the verse contrasts three words, 'power', 'perfect' and 'weakness'. Whatever Paul may have meant by weakness, the word has tended to possess a different meaning in the hands of theologians and preachers. It is such a powerful phrase that it must be salvaged from the 'weakness' of other interpretations. It must also not become a burden unless it is chosen as such in the same way as one has to choose to 'take up the Cross'. A cross that is not lifted voluntarily is not worth lifting nor can a weakness be exploited if it either is a term of abuse or is misunderstood. Many people in history have extolled the virtues of weakness in the face of brute force. The crucifixion is the Christian example of the supreme weakness of Jesus being overwhelmed by the power of the Roman state and the brutality of the Roman soldiers being turned to good in the resurrection. Ghandi is also a model of a man who turned the weakness of civil disobedience against the injustice of the British administration in India into strength of moral protest and incontestable power. The important thing to notice is that to act weakly in fact required enormous strength of character and of organisation. 'Weakness' in this sense of the word is not weakness, and although Paul spoke of it as such, he required great fortitude to bear his 'thorn in the flesh' and although the weakness was apparent to others it required strength of him to continue his ministry with such an affliction.

The word 'weakness' has been used by many to contradict the very strong egalitarianism that is contained in his doctrine of the body of Christ. The word is indeed biblical and comes from 1 Corinthians 12:22: '... those parts of the body that seem to be weaker are indispensable'. Its proper use will be discussed below but we must note that it has become a word which can become a term which can be used to objectify people with disabilities. It has been used in this way by many church people, the *World Council of Churches* (WCC) and has been applied to weaker churches as if they were in some way disabled. The WCC has a sad history of over thirty years of describing disabled people as objects but this has been amended by the publication of an *Interim Statement*, 'A Church of All and for All'. (Reprinted in Fritzson and Kabue, 2004: p 64ff). A correct understanding would stress that there is no weakness in any part of the body of Christ, simply a variety of functions, which tend to be hierarchical, but of equal value.

This doctrine makes it clear that every part of the body is equal, or at least equally dependent on the others, and no distinction is made between the parts except for some which are considered unseemly and which modesty compels us to cover. It is surely misguided to talk of certain organs being weaker than others are. The heart is obviously more important than our appendix but both must be healthy to contribute to the well being of the human body. If certain disabled people are to be considered weaker, it must only be in a similar context. A Christian community that does not value them is allowing part of the body to deteriorate in a way that will make the whole both weaker and unhealthy. It is not a good idea to suggest that weakness is a quality of disability and to relegate disabled people to a secondary place in the community as a result.

Now we turn to the ways in which the 'thorn' has been given significance in the general scheme of theology. Wilkinson (1998; chapter 19) argues strongly that 'the thorn in the flesh' has global implications for our understanding of illness. He rightly begins from the understanding that there is no definitive explanation of Paul's affliction. Wilkinson then argues that the way Paul deals with his situation gives us a general explanation of illness and of God's dealing with those who are ill. The immediate problem that occurs is that we believe that disabled people are not looking for explanations but for ways that ameliorate their lives. An explanation of an illness does not do this and is reactive rather than proactive. Wilkinson suggests that Paul accepted that the 'thorn in the flesh' had been given by God and although it was not the work of Satan, Satan could turn it to his own purpose. However, he was unable to do so because the 'thorn' created its own positive attitude in Paul teaching him the meaning of humility, acceptance through prayer and gave him strength of character that carried him through many trials. Illness or disability is not given by God in order to build character. We do not live in 'a vale of soul-making' (Hick, 1977) in which we are redeemed and shaped into more God, or Christ-like characters by our response to suffering.

> In the hour of pain and suffering, Christians can know that their experience is not an accident outside the purpose of God resulting from a suspension of his providence, but a situation in which God is active for good with everything under his control. From this we can draw encouragement and reassurance as we face our own experience

of illness and suffering, and follow the example of Paul and seek healing and strength from the Lord. (Wilkinson, 1998; p 235)

In this, Wilkinson is mistaken. The gifts of disabled people emerge as they reach their full potential as barriers are broken down in a partnership with other people in the fellowship of Christ. (Monteith, 2005; p 214f) Wilkinson's model has no doubt been adopted by many disabled people but has been rejected by many more. It is also a glamorisation of disability and of people with disabilities in that he suggests that from illness all the qualities of strength and steadfastness in prayer can be learnt. So be it, but this in turn leads to a glamorization of disabled people as possessing all these desirable qualities as Christians when, in fact, they may be very average and sinners like everyone else.

There is no overall model or explanation of illness which can be drawn out of Paul's 'thorn in the flesh' because what we have in the letters and the biographical reports by Luke in the Acts of the Apostles represents a deeply personal reflection on one man's conversion and subsequent mission in the face of an obstacle which seemed to plague him. It would be wrong to end on a negative note by suggesting that there is no universal meaning to the 'thorn in the flesh'. The important point is such meaning must be intrinsic to oneself as a disabled person and not imposed from outside.

Søren Kierkegaard gives us a good example in view of the fact that he is known as the father of Christian existentialism and fought to assert the value of the inner struggle of a Christian to gain faith despite all odds. As he fought with his 'thorn in the flesh', he realised the potential for personal development, for a deeper understanding of his own inner being and psyche. It has been suggested that such a struggle is necessary in everyone who wishes to understand and release the full power of their potential. It is said of Kierkegaard, and others who fight similar irritations, '... that he subordinates all his desires and his whole life to God's will, and thereby helps him to practice one of the most important of the religious virtues'. (Hong, 2003; p 115)

Anyone with the dedication of Paul can, as Paul did with the help of his friends in Galatia who offered their own eyes to relieve Paul's suffering (Galatians 4:15), find ways to overcome and grow in the face of a 'thorn in the flesh'. However, in the case of people with disabilities the outcome of this struggle will depend on the degree to which societal barriers may be removed by a willing and receptive Christian fellowship. Such a fellowship allows the gifts of individuals to blossom, not because of adversity, but because they have been afforded many opportunities to grow beyond the limits imposed by any 'thorn in the flesh'.

Chapter Two

The Apostles' Ministry of Healing

Accounts of miraculous healing was not confined to those of Jesus in the Gospels but continue throughout the rest of the New Testament.

Saint Paul

In the last chapter, we saw how Paul lived with a menacing 'thorn in the flesh' which may have been an impairment that would count as a disability. He found comfort in people's understanding of his problem and also drew strength from the statement he believed it made about his faith and his relationship to God. In this chapter, the search for Paul's understanding of disability turns to the consideration of two questions: 1) how did this ministry or attitude compare to that of Jesus; and, 2) did Paul consider that he had a ministry to disabled people and those in need of healing?

Paul came from a very different background from Jesus. Jesus was born and brought up in a radical part of Israel, Nazareth and around the Sea of Galilee where poverty was rife and discontent with the current rulers was the norm. His ministry had freshness and a radicalism which other firebrands of the time lacked. His was an apocalyptic vision and ministry which included an imperative to heal in fulfilment of the prophecy of Isaiah chapter 35 of which verses 5 and 6 need be quoted:

> 5 Then will the eyes of the blind be opened
> and the ears of the deaf unstopped.
>
> 6 Then will the lame leap like a deer,
> and the mute tongue shout for joy.

Jesus took this prophecy literally and not metaphorically and went out of his way to help and to heal people with such impairments.

One noticeable difference between him and Paul is that people began to learn to come to Jesus to be healed whilst Paul tended to heal and to talk about those who are sick within his communities of converted Christians. If Paul was concerned about the apocalyptic signs of healing, he did not appear to stress it. His concern for those around him who were ill tended to be a natural and genuine concern for friends and colleagues who often had what we would now consider common diseases such as diarrhoea, which was probably more serious in his time and climate as it still is in parts of the developing world. Jesus reflected about his healings and taught from them whereas with one notable exception, Paul offered no such explanation or teaching about the love and nature of God. The only time when Paul does connect a passage about healers to a broad statement of the meaning of God's love is in 1 Corinthians 13 after listing healing as a gift of the Spirit in chapter 12. Jesus took tremendous risks to heal and because he taught from his healings that sin was not the prime cause of illness, he offended many including the party of the Pharisees to which Saul belonged. Paul does not seem to take such risks.

If Paul had a message about healing it was that it was based upon the virtues that came from the Spirit. This indeed is very different of the message of Jesus but equally exciting to a Church which was moving into its second phase, or as Hans Küng puts it a second paradigm in which Hellenistic influences predominate (Küng & Tracy, 1998), a phase when the Church had not witnessed the anticipated and imminent second coming and adapted its theology accordingly. Paul's compassion was great but lacked the urgency of that of Jesus who expected to show in his ministry the dawning of God's kingdom which is a word lacking in Paul's vocabulary.

Paul's ministry was different in other ways. The Apostles, Peter and James, had healed in the Name of Jesus (Acts 3) whereas Paul seldom uttered the formula that attributed the miracle to Jesus. In addition, as we shall see, Paul is the first person in the New Testament to inflict blindness on another as a divine punishment for sorcery. (Acts 13:6–12)

Thus to the second question – what constituted Paul's ministry to the sick and disabled. It must be repeated what Paul was chiefly concerned with those who were in his own community. In 1 Timothy chapter 5, Paul offers detailed advice on many aspects of welfare including the proper behaviour for widows and advice on how to treat old people with respect, but then goes on to say:

> Do not be hasty in the laying on of hands, and do not share in the sins of others. Keep yourself pure.

> 23 Stop drinking only water, and use a little wine because of your stomach and your frequent illnesses. (James 5: 22 & 23)

The words about healing are totally different from the gospel words; they do not make up a separate story and seemed to be tagged on to a whole list of advice without any miraculous content. It is well known that Paul's advice about wine was absolutely correct and yet he ties it into the ritual of laying on of hands which he cautions must not be overdone or indulged in too often. Paul's advice is so different from Jesus, Peter and James.

Most of the records of Paul's concern with illness are written by Luke in the Acts of the Apostles, some record this matter of fact everyday type of involvement with illness whilst others obviously have a teaching role in the same way as some of the healing miracles of Jesus. Luke records Paul's involvement with everyday illnesses in Malta without making a great theological point and he stresses that many Maltese went to see Paul in order to be cured. These healings were done in the name of Christ, but were so written that they stress the power of God through Paul himself.

Most of Paul's miracles as related by Luke do have a didactic purpose behind them. In many of his travels, Paul visited areas where magic and sorcery were rife. Such areas included Ephesus and many other areas including Malta. Paul performs signs and wonders in these regions in an attempt to defeat the power of the sorcerers. The principle story concerns Elymas who sought to perform miracles by magic. Paul in the presence of the governor of Cyprus struck Elymas blind; it is not known whether it was temporary or permanent, as punishment for his abuse by magic of the healing process. Luke may well have felt that a polemic had to be fought against such magicians after he was impressed by the healing miracles of Jesus and of the Apostles.

This is more than an interesting point to note *en route* but is an important introduction to the most fascinating part of Paul's involvement with healing and possibly with disability. Paul went on his missionary journeys to attempt to set up ideal communities of Christians. These Christians were converted to the new faith and initiated into the fellowship by baptism. (Carlson, 1993) It also conferred a degree of equality on all members of the new Christian communities. It gave them all the rights of mature and adult Christian who were drawn from either a Gentile background or Jewish synagogues with a Greek background that tends to make them more liberal than their Hebrew counterparts. Paul was painfully aware that the communities that he founded were not prefect but he certainly looked for perfection. This was expressed in the gifts of the Spirit, which came from God and reflected the mind of Christ; these were of the highest virtue and probably an adaptation of the virtues that groups like the Cynics already sought in their lives. Healing could not be allowed to be cheapened by magic nor allowed to be so debased that they had no value at all. Healing was to be part of the community but not an end in itself. Whilst Paul often sought to dampen down the enthusiasm of the employment of the gifts of the spirit so that it did not detract from the real point (1 Corinthians 13:1), it was undoubtedly the case that these newfound gifts and virtues were tremendously important to these early Christians.

The initial reception of the Spirit among Pauline Christians entailed at least potentially knowing the mind of the Lord, "having the mind of Christ". But behaviourally it involved rather more, it involved speaking with tongues, prophesying and healing. (Downing, 1998; p 220)

These spiritual qualities mark the first important feature of the burgeoning Christian communities, but there is a second equally important characteristic, that of being a community based or house church. Segal (1990) makes this a central point in his argument that these communities were groups of converted individuals who believed that their uniqueness lay in their faith in their risen Christ. It may well have been that Paul might have preferred to reform the synagogues but this was not to be. His communities were tight-knit groups of people drawn together by faith and worshipping in small groups in towns and regions that often had very different values.

The secret of inclusiveness lay in the structure of these groups. The sick and disabled were amongst them as indeed they are within any family. Accidents happened within these groups and people were smitten with ordinary everyday diseases as described in Philipians 2:25–27. Here, in his own words, Paul describes the effect the illness of Epaphroditus had on the morale and concerns of the community. Luke also records an instance where we find healing integrated into an obvious example of a house church. (Segal, 1990; p 171ff) It was common in the early church to worship during the night and in Acts 20:7–12 we are given a perfect example of how Christians gathered to worship, break bread and to learn until dawn. It has been suggested that 'Hail gladdening light' may well have been one of the earliest hymns reflecting the dawning of a new day, both spiritually and in reality. In this instance, we learn that Paul talked on and on until a young boy, Eutychus fell from the window ledge on which he was sitting because he had fallen asleep – something which most Christians have experienced! Paul revived him in a way that was reminiscent of Elijah and then went on preaching. This miracle is marked by both a humour and a locus within the worshipping community, which makes it very different from similar miracles in the gospels. Healing and acceptance of illness was within the community of believers. It had become inclusive of all.

When Paul does talk of healing, it is within the context of the gifts of the spirit and with a cautioned call for moderation. He is almost saying that disabled people and people who are sick are part of the community and any gifts of virtues that people have must be exercised in an inclusive way. In 1 Cor:12:28 & 29, he writes:

> And in the church God has appointed first of all apostles, second prophets, third teachers, then workers of miracles, also those having gifts of healing, those able to help others, those with gifts of administration, and those speaking in different kinds of tongues.

Here he makes a distinction between miracles and healing which remains unexplained but seems to suggest that healing was part of the work of a faithful community whereas miracles covered many types of signs. In the verse that immediate follows this, Paul yet again dampens expectations possibly to keep activities such as healing under control just as he accused the Corinthians of abusing the Lord's Supper by over indulging in food and drink. Paul's communities were indeed inclusive; and in aim at least sought to be the perfect communities in which the body of Christ could prosper.

In the light of modern experience, it is possible envisage a community where disabled people are accepted as an integral part of the larger body. L'Arche communities are one such example where at every stage in their development disabled people are accommodated and valued for their own true worth as members of the body of Christ. This will be dealt with in a later chapter.

Likewise, there is a very real sense in which no Christian should suffer alone. To be alone is a negation of every value that a Christian should have. Common daily concern for the sick and disabled in our midst is central to every churches' liturgy but some are better at the practice than others are. It is at this point that we must turn to the letter of James to illustrate an example of how the New Testament came to have such concerns at its centre.

Letter of James

The letter of James illustrates most clearly how the early Church regarded healing and took their responsibilities to the sick seriously. It is useful in the context of an inclusive community to understand what the Church demanded of its members and particularly its elders. It is clear that people with an illness were not to be neglected but offered help as a priority by other church members.

This letter was probably written by the brother of Jesus but this very fact throws up the first puzzle. Healing as described by James in his letter is something that is very formal, is dependent upon prayer and involved ritual anointing with oil. It was not the type of healing which Jesus himself undertook. Jesus sought out disabled people and as the Bible put it, he cured them. Whatever he did, he gave them a fresh understanding of themselves, their relationship to others and a new freedom from the constraints of disability that usually entailed social exclusion and a life of begging. James has already began to refine the meaning of healing and to offer a ritual which was available to the early Christian Church. The marked departure from the practice of Jesus shows yet again the maturing of the early church and the move away from healing as an apocalyptic sign. The early church very quickly began to owe loyalty to individual leaders who became 'resident' in communities of established Christians. These leaders included Paul, James and Peter and between them, they began to establish the rudiments of church order on which practices could be built. (Horrell, 1997)

James wrote the letter as one of these leaders encouraging people to 'walk as Christ did' and to put into practice the knowledge of how he lived and the imperatives of the faith he engendered. Although this is the pattern of most letters of Paul and others, Moo (2000) has suggested that the entire letter might have been a sermon or homily to a certain group of people. The reception of the letter over the centuries has been mixed with the Reformers showing a distinct dislike for it because it seems to encourage acts before faith. The letter certainly is an encouragement to the faithful of the time to serve each other and the wider community.

James' comments about healing have had a major influence on the Church even although they only occupy a few verses of the five chapters of the letter.

Is any one of you in trouble? He should pray. Is anyone happy? Let him sing songs of praise. 14 Is any one of you sick? He should call the elders of the church to pray over him and anoint him with oil in the name of the Lord. 15 And the prayer offered in faith will make the sick person well; the Lord will raise him up. If he has sinned, he will be forgiven. 16 Therefore confess your sins to each other and pray for each other so that you may be healed. The prayer of a righteous man is powerful and effective.

These verses come after a section that deals with the need for compassion and patience whilst waiting for the Lord to come. James had a particular concern for social justice, as had many of the Old Testament prophets; and when his advice moves on to healing, he begins to concentrate upon prayer and forgiveness. (Hartin, 1999)

There are five features of healing highlighted in these verses. First, there is an implicit assumption that the people know whom the elders of the Church are and can make easy contact with them. This contact implies that people can be confident that they may have a formal but intimate relationship with the elders in the context of healing. Second, the elders are enjoined to pray and to anoint with oil. No more is asked of them. Third, the only ritual the elders are asked to indulge in is anointing with oil, which has generally been interpreted as a formal anointing rather that the application of ointment or medicine to a wound or treat a particular symptom. Fourth, there is a discussion about forgiveness of sins, which may, or may not, be related to illness, but certainly implies some communal activity and mutual accounting. Last, James spells out the expectations he has of elders, namely that they are righteous and faithful. Without these qualities, their prayers will be in vain.

In the Church of today, there is not such an inclusiveness engendered by the training and expectation of elders (or any of the other interpretations of presbutevrou" or presbyters). There is a growing trend of appointing 'pastoral assistants' in congregations who visit and help the housebound or lonely, but there is not the injunction to heal in the way in which the early elders were expected to. However, it is at this point that the interpretation of 'presbyters' becomes problematic because some may regard them as ministers either at the time of James or in present congregations. This debate is probably impossible to resolve but congregations must develop that degree of inclusiveness that was implied in the early church.

There are three features of James' advice about healing that should be considered in more detail. Besides the fact that the Christian community was called to visit the sick not only by elders but also by all concerned members of the community, the inclusiveness of the new Christianity was underlined by the nature of healing. The three most important features are prayer itself, anointing and mutual confession. They will be considered separately but taken together they underline a belief that everyone who is part of the Christian community has a value both in the sight of God and within the fellowship of God's people.

Prayer

Lack of belief in prayer is perhaps the greatest obstacle to healing today. Medicine has taken over as the most important way of finding relief from an illness or disability and prayer has been relegated to a support for the work of doctors and other medical staff. At the time of Jesus and of James, prayer, or a right relationship to God was far more important than one's relationship to a physician. Jesus underlined this in several of his comments and most notably in the story of the miracle of healing a boy who had no speech and was probably epileptic, in chapter 9 of Mark's gospel, where, in response to the debate that ensued, Jesus said, 'This kind can come out only by prayer'. (Mk 9:29) Here his brother James takes up the same theme suggesting that a prayer of faith was a prerequisite of any healing. Several authors have argued that it had to be a prayer of a certain quality of faith that is lacking today – hence the lack of healing today – but still there are many who believe in modern healing services and the laying on of hands. Wilkinson reminds us that 'laying on of hands' was not prescribed by James and by implication suggests that our modern practices are suspect. (Wilkinson, 1998, p 244ff) He further points out that in Luke's writing in Acts and in James, the emphasis was upon the collective power of healing not on particular individuals as it is today. The entire leadership might be called upon. The prayer that was uttered had to come from a righteous believer, which reinforces the idea that elders, although they were members of the general Christian community, had to be gifted by a certain spiritual quality for the prayers to be effective. Keith Warrington argues that the direct healing of Jesus was unique and had a specific mission behind it. He goes on to suggest that all later church workers who prayed for and exercized gifts of healing were qualitatively different and depended upon the type of formula set out in James. The quality of their prayer was of supreme importance and even then, they had no right to expect healing results. (Warrington, 2000; p 150ff) This very strict interpretation seems to fly in the face of many healing services today where the entire congregation is invited to take part without any prior examination of their ability to do so. In one of the most prominent healing services of today, that of the Iona Community, there has been a progressive move since 1938 to allow more and more people to take part in the service. In 1938, the service was restricted to those who had the gift of healing and to others who were ordained, whereas today, everyone is invited to take part. (See Introduction by Monteith, 'The Healing Service of the Iona Community' in Burgess & Galloway, 2000)

Anointing with oil

Wilkinson has many valuable points to make about anointing. Anointing with oil was not considered to have much medicinal value. The application of olive oil in the name of Christ was considered to enhance the chances of recovery and to support the healing process. In the context of James, it signified the special relationship a sick person had with God as anointing had always done in the Old Testament. Previous chapters of James show the influence of the Old Testament on his thought and this extends to anointing. (Hartin, 2003)

For a long period of Christian history, anointing was associated with the onset of death. The gospel tradition illustrates the woman going to the tomb where Jesus lay with oil to anoint him and most interpretation of the story of Mary Magdalene wiping Jesus' feet with her tears and pouring expensive nard, aromatic oil, on him is that she is prefiguring his death with this anointing very close to the liturgy of 'Holy Week'. The Roman Catholic Church developed the idea of anointing as the 'last rite', it became engrained in our culture and countless generations of nurses became used to calling a priest to a deathbed. The *Second Vatican Council* (1962–65) attempted to turn this sacrament into one for 'anointing of the sick' but it was never a very successful move and any use of oil in the context of healing services has always rested uneasily on the minds of Reformed congregations.

Within the Reformed tradition, anointing with oil has become an integral part of modern healing services. Sometimes it is offered in addition to the laying on of hands; on other occasions, it is used as an alternative. Members of the congregation step forward and the minister places a drop of oil on their forehead with a word of blessing to accompany the act. It can be a most inclusive experience having a moment of the service entirely devoted to you and to receiving the prayers and attention of the congregation. The anointing is a symbol representing always the marking of a special concern of the people of God for the sick within their midst. The oil is offered in the faith that God will act as the instrument of healing as the person is dedicated to his beneficent purpose. The act may have been more private in the time of James but its effect was exactly the same. The recipient was gathered by the congregation and committed to God's care and special attention by the elder who brought this gift with him.

Confession of Sins

Verse 16 is a very important verse in the instructions that James offers because it deals with sin in the context of illness. It also instructs the small Christian community to act together in confessing their sins. It calls for a degree of mutuality, which underlines the whole idea of an inclusive community of faith. It is worth repeating the verse:

> Therefore confess your sins to each other and pray for each other so that you may be healed.

It is correctly argued by most commentators that Jesus never connected sin with people with disabilities or an illness. Whenever someone came to him for healing, he never suggested that their sins should be forgiven and, in fact, chose to suggest that forgiving sins was too easy and showed a facile understanding of God's working. As Warrington (2000) points out the only instance when Jesus actually accused someone of sin was when he told the woman found in adultery to sin no more. He never asked for confession of sins from a disabled or sick person as a *quid pro quo* for healing. This raises the question of why sin is now associated with illness by James – and to a lesser extent Paul?

The first thing to notice is that James is making both sin and confession into a very social act. The individual is almost secondary to the community and the mutuality of confession becomes terribly important. We are not told what they are to confess and the sins that have been committed have not been described in any detail. It is entirely possible that James shared with his brother, Jesus, the same attitude to sin which was founded in good common sense. Sin throughout the Old Testament had been backed by separation and banishment from the nearness of God that was found in the rituals of the time and the religious expressions of the community. Nevertheless, when Jesus encountered people with disabilities; he generally met someone who was socially disenfranchized and condemned to begging or expulsion because of fear of contagion or demons that manifested themselves in disruptive behaviour. Sin in this context was as much an offence to society as to God, if not more so. Such sin was firmly rooted in folk traditions of shame and disgrace, which would be gossiped about, and subject to judgment by many voices in the community. (Pilch, 1995 & 2000) By talking about it in a forgiving and newly found Christian way (Jones, 2000), James was suggesting that health could actually be promoted. He was suggesting that people could find a new relationship with God that was always essential prior to receiving healing either from the community or from physicians. He was further making the radical proposal that the new Christian community had within it the power to give to each other mutual understanding of their problems and the worries that might often lead to disease or to the isolation of sufferers.

We have here an early example of the 'priesthood of all believers'. James was encouraging freedom amongst all to minister to each other and to draw strength from their faith, not by always looking to the hierarchy, but looking inwards to their own strength as a fellowship of faith. Confession is about health and as McNeill points out, it has tremendous therapeutic value:

> What is potentially the most important phase of the Lutheran personal ministry has been the cultivation ... of the mutual cure of souls on the part of laymen. Each man was his brother's keeper in a spiritual fellowship, "*Seelsorge aller an allen*" (the care of all for the souls of all), aptly expresses this principle. (McNeill 1952: p 190)

The doctrine, which became a watchword of the Reformation, the priesthood of all believers, can be found working in the community that James was trying to build. With it comes a new chapter in the responsibility of people of faith to look out for one another and to offer spiritual help as well as this practical help that many have assumed was James' most serious intent.

Letter to the Hebrews

An examination of the Letter to the Hebrews is perhaps a bigger digression from the subject of this book than even the Letter of James. Healing is a process which is far larger than curing or offering succour to those who are ill or disabled. Some would say that healing must be an escape from the sentimentality which could be read into the previous sentence. Others would argue that healing is not about illness at all but about the process of becoming whole through the development of an identity or a healthy personality or a wholesome place in society. All these three examples are part of our understanding of healing but the lack of them stems from an alienation which can be felt as a deep social pain by individuals or by groups who are marginalized within society. Authors such as Eiesland have shown a way out of this by appropriating religious symbols to their own situation as people with disabilities. It has now become the most important aspect of disability consciousness as people become aware of the barriers which are placed before them. Disabled people are created and retained by a society that can be deeply alienating.

Hebrews represents a supreme example of how a group of Christians overcame their feelings of alienation through their understanding of the triumph of Christ against the forces that crushed the good which had been exemplified in his life and ministry. They did so by creating new symbols drawn from an exegesis of the Old Testament and relating it to the New. The Hebrews were a group who were pilgrims seeking reassurance that their symbols gave their lives wholesome meaning and a freedom from the alienation which not only existed in their new found Christian faith but in the very implications of these symbols.

The authorship of the letter is unknown. The Church Father, Origen, declared that God alone knew who the author was. When the Bible became codified and took on a greater unity, it became known as 'St Paul's Letter to the Hebrews', which was in all likelihood far from accurate but as Manson (1966) mentions *en passent*, there is a slim possibility that the letter may represent a development of Paul's theology long after the New Testament leaves him in Rome. This is attractive but unlikely. Equally so is the suggestion, again by Manson that the letter was written by a group of conservative Christians who wanted to preserve the priesthood of Jesus above all else. It is, however, more likely that it was written to a group of Christian who were deeply troubled by their new found faith which seemed to fly in the face of their Jewish background and threw up anomalies which were perplexing to a group eager to find an expression of their faith. The Hebrews represent a group of early Christians who are not unlike minority groups now who must find an expression of their faith in the face of all that discourages them.

The real problem was Jesus and the manner of his death. By any standard, crucifixion was scandalous and could not be tolerated except by people who worked through the scandal to an understanding of the Christ who was resurrected at the end of it. There are several key texts but the most important is Hebrews 13:11–15 which comes as almost like a crescendo at the end of a letter of torturous theological reasoning:

> 11 The high priest carries the blood of animals into the Most Holy Place as a sin offering, but the bodies are burned outside the camp.

> 12 And so Jesus also suffered outside the city gate to make the people holy through his own blood.

> 13 Let us, then, go to him outside the camp, bearing the disgrace he bore.

> 14 For here we do not have an enduring city, but we are looking for the city that is to come.

> 15 Through Jesus, therefore, let us continually offer to God a sacrifice of praise—the fruit of lips that confess his name

Their triumph was a triumph over disgrace – the disgrace of following a Saviour who has triumphed over the disgrace of being put to death outside the city on the rubbish dump on a gibbet which had always been taken to be a sign, from Leviticus, that God had deserted anyone so put to death. In order to come to terms with this disgrace, these new Christians must follow Jesus and offer their worship as they progress their pilgrimage towards the eternal city which could now exist outwith the establishment centred in Jerusalem. The disgrace represented their alienation; their willingness to embrace it was their key to their glorious identity in Christ.

Their pilgrimage was not one embarked on in the dark. They had countless witnesses from the Old Testament who had gone forth in faith or had been saved from some fate by their faith. Chapter 11 of the letter is a catalogue of all the heroes of the Old Testament who had sallied forth in faith and now it is their turn to follow the example of Christ. There is yet one more ingredient to add to their story of a search for wholeness, an escape from the alienation of Christ's own disgrace. Christ is given an obscure status derived from an Old Testament character who is mentioned but twice in all the books. This character is the priest, Melchizedek, who is understood to have prefigured Christ in the Old Testament and now becomes the symbol of the order which Christ has inherited by fiat of his Father. Melchizedek is first seen as an early king in Genesis 14 and also as a priest who shared bread and wine in a way which some denominations have interpreted an early Eucharist of the style instituted by Jesus. He next appears in Psalm 110:4 as a priest which has become a recognised style in the Old Testament. By the time we come to Hebrews, Melchizedek represents an order of priesthood, the name of which is only worthy to be associated with Jesus who is God's High Priest for ever. (Thomas, 2000)

> 11 If perfection could have been attained through the Levitical priesthood (for on the basis of it the law was given to the people), why was there still need for another priest to come—one in the order of Melchizedek, not in the order of Aaron? 15 And what we have said is even more clear if another priest like Melchizedek appears, 17 For it is declared:
>
> "You are a priest forever,
>
> in the order of Melchizedek" (Heb.7:11–17)

There is a strange tension and contradiction in Hebrew between the perfection of Melchizedek and the imperfection of the death of Jesus on the Cross. As pilgrims, they moved forward guided by the perfect High Priest Christ but motivated by the understanding that they must undergo the same indignity as Jesus. They were journeying to and through death outside the city in search of the eternal one. This constitutes the perfect example of how a people can adopt symbols which overcome their alienation and their lack of status to find an expression of faith which meets their social situation which may have been very hard. (See Salevao, 2002, whose study shows how the letter can address the particular social situation of this group of Christians.) Salevao shows how hope can arise for distress of a group seeking to make sense of their deeply disturbing faith in the freshness of the application of exciting new symbols.

Manson sums up the general view that suggests an escape from the stifling past to an exciting future:

> ... that the Temple-worship, the sacrifices, the Law, all the holy institutions of the past, were thereby transcended and antiquated, and that *the call to the Church of Jesus was to leave the Temple and all that went with it behind, and to go forward* , no longer clinging to historical securities, no longer thinking to capitalise the grace of God in the Jewish ordinances and cultus, but throwing in its lot with the crucified Son of Man, to whom the throne of the world and the Lordship of the Age to Come belonged? (Manson, 1966; p 32)

This group of Christians were left with an opportunity, as were those who followed Paul, to grow fluid and inclusive communities that were only threatened by the growing institutionalization of the post-Constantine church.

... ...

This chapter and the last have highlighted the way in which the Apostles developed a care for those who had any kind of illness within in their midst. Quite a number of the pastoral epistles which have not been mentioned in these chapters make sufficient reference to the 'laying on of hands' to show that they too had a concern. Paul experienced the wonder of being cared for twice: first, at the time of his conversion; and second, when the Galatians were deeply concerned for his health. He in turn spoke of the need to care for those who required healing and he offered healing himself in various contexts.

In the general scheme of things, there was little apparent need for the writers of these letters to spend any time discussing illness. The church and beliefs had moved on from the urgency with which Jesus healed and the whole matter could have been lost in the development of doctrines that were to carry the Church forward for centuries. Yet at the heart of all the writings are communities of faithful people who could not avoid illness and disability but had to address a painful and unpleasant fact. By making disability and illness important, they illustrated how inclusive their doctrines had to be and it is now time to examine how these doctrines carried the cause of disability forward.

Part Two

Community and the Body

Chapter Three

The Body of Christ

To recap on the previous two chapters, it can be said that Paul and other Apostles had a concern to build communities in which everyone who had faith could be incorporated. Paul was severely restricted by his 'thorn in the flesh' and in all probability had to fight for acceptance but turned that fight into an added dimension of his faith and his determination to spread his understanding of the gospel throughout the communities he visited. He wrote with a conviction that 'his' people accepted him and assisted with physical support at the time of his conversion and moral support when he faced what we assumed to be illness and which he called his 'thorn in the flesh'.

Unlike the ministry of Jesus, Paul and the other apostles did not heal out of a missionary or messianic conviction; but out of a desire to ensure that everyone was included in the community of faith. This resulted sometimes in miraculous cures but in the majority of cases members of the community were assured that they were loved and cared for and healed by prayer and laying on of hands. James, notably, urged anointing with oil as a supplement to medical care.

The next three chapters will look at some of Paul's most important doctrines and practices which were not directly concerned with health or with healing but encouraged an inclusion which has continued to this day, or not as the case may be. This chapter will describe the doctrine of the body of Christ and the values it, and baptism, instilled in the community, whilst the next two will look at what might be called their 'derivatives'. What barriers have the churches erected to full participation in the eucharist and the enjoyment of the rights of baptism? Some visionaries, notably Jean Vanier, have attempted to build inclusive communities modelled on the implications of the Body of Christ. This will be the subject of the last chapter in this section.

Ideas and ideologies, with very few exceptions other than those of Hitler and a few others, start with good and lofty intentions that are gradually corrupted by practice and interpretation. The intentions of Karl Marx in writing *The Communist Manifesto* are hard to criticise until one remembers that Stalin interpreted it in a very cruel and sadistic way. At the level of the general populace, Marxism did not lead to the high moral values that might have been expected but to amorality, at best, and immorality at worst. Paul's doctrines have some times suffered the same fate as theologians have deliberated upon them and passed on to Christendom. Dogmatic theology has always reflected the needs and interests of the Church of the time. These pronouncements become traditions that have caused hurt to disabled people and to other minorities as well.

This chapter will ultimately look at the Body of Christ as a perfect description of a Christian community. This will be briefly preceded by a look at Paul's attitude to equality and the role of baptism as the universal symbol of acceptance and adoption by the fellowship of faith. The importance of the symbolic participation in the Lord's Supper will be considered. Later on, certain of the phrases used will begin to unravel to reveal potential hurts and exclusions from mainstream Christianity.

Equality in Faith

The text, which is most commonly quoted in support of equality amongst all Christians, comes from Galatians 3:28:

> There is neither Jew nor Greek, slave nor free, male nor female, for you are all one in Christ Jesus.

Paul's community of Christians was one linked by a common bond of baptism. Within that bond, the laws of the Old Testament were redundant, but outside of it, these same laws were indispensable. People lived by grace that was given by the spirit imparted at baptism. Paul can be called an universalist, not in the usual way of talking of salvation being available to everyone, but because he was the first Christian to suggest that everyone could break free from the shackles of the law and live in an universal state of grace and equality *in* faith. This fact means that all law can now be based on its availability to all and not a particular group as in the case of the Old Testament. (Badiou, 2003) That 'in', in the section heading 'Equality in Faith', is important because Paul was not an egalitarian as Marx and many revolutionaries since have been but promoted the idea of equality under or in faith for all who were baptized in the name of Christ. Despite this verse, slavery continued for another eighteen centuries and woman's rights only began to take off in the last century. Paul uses the metaphor of slavery to describe and explain the past before Christ. We were 'slaves' to sin and to the law and our freedom was limited and circumvented by our obedience to those laws. Pharisees, like Paul, were particular 'slaves' to the law and the ritual observance that filled up the day with prayers and washing and choice of food. Therefore, it would seem that Paul used the word 'slave' in a particular way but this verse was not referring to their status in the case of slaves or their station in the case of women but to their absolute equality in their right to worship God in their newfound state of grace. This is not to decry the equality, which was implied by the statement, because Jews and Gentiles would no longer be distinguished by circumcision but the equality was still limited by social convention and necessity. In Paul's term, the physically manifest covenant was replaced by a spiritual covenant with God.

The early Church was already becoming hierarchical as the fame of the apostles appointed them to positions of authority that they delegated to others. These others were men; women had to wait many centuries to be offered positions in the Church. Their positions changed in many denominations not because of any doctrinal reversal or deviation but because they were no longer the social conventions which had thwarted their power in the earlier years. In the secular world, woman had been enfranchised and liberated. This same argument can be applied to other minority groups including disabled people because social convention now dictates that there should be no discrimination on the grounds of given differences. This is where I feel that the situation differs with gays and lesbians because it is hard to argue that their sexuality is given and devoid of choice. Christians must still decide on this issue and their place in equality legislation throughout the western world tends to confuse and dilute the attention given people with disabilities whose differences are given facts of their birth or accident – facts that cannot be changed.

Baptism

In baptism, all the apostles sealed all Christians in a mystical bond, which implied equality before Christ, and demanded mutual respect from each member to another. When Peter was called to minister to Cornelius in the 10th chapter of Acts he found himself drawn into a new situation where he was challenged on the issue of dietary laws and came to realise their irrelevance in the face of the new faith and law of grace in Jesus Christ. When he baptized Cornelius, he summed up the whole idea of equality in the following verse:

> Then Peter began to speak: "I now realize how true it is that God does not show favouritism". (Acts 10:34)

The equality, which was implicit in baptism, receives further testimony in Acts in that it was offered to crowds of penitent listeners or to people of high office such as the Ethiopian eunuch. (Acts 8:26–40)

Paul explains baptism as initiating a mystical union with Christ that is instilled in his followers Christ's life was noted for his death on the cross, it was a stumbling block and a folly, yet through it came life. The victory over death was central to Paul's thought and preaching which proclaimed victory to all who believed. As a theory, this was barely understandable but given the mystery of baptism at the beginning of a Christian's journey through faith, it became a living reality and the key to true membership of the community of faith.

For in Christ all the fullness of the Deity lives in bodily form, 10 and you have been given fullness in Christ, who is the head over every power and authority. 11 In him you were also circumcised, in the putting off of the sinful nature, not with a circumcision done by the hands of men but with the circumcision done by Christ, 12 having been buried with him in baptism and raised with him through your faith in the power of God, who raised him from the dead.

13 When you were dead in your sins and in the uncircumcision of your sinful nature, God made you alive with Christ. He forgave us all our sins, 14 having cancelled the written code, with its regulations, that was against us and that stood opposed to us; he took it away, nailing it to the cross. 15 And having disarmed the powers and authorities, he made a public spectacle of them, triumphing over them by the cross. (Col.2:9–15)

This passage makes it clear that baptism has supplanted circumcision as a physical sign of God's covenant with his people by a spiritual sign of baptism that was available to Jew and Gentile alike and in a spiritual equality. Baptism was to become the supreme symbol of assent and adoption into the Christian community. The total immersion into water signified a death as if by drowning and a re-emergence into the full spiritual life in which Christ now lived and to which he called his followers. Just as Jesus overcame the powers of the Roman state, Paul eloquently puts it in Romans that baptized Christians enjoy the same support from God in chapter 8:

For I am convinced that neither death nor life, neither angels nor demons, neither the present nor the future, not any powers, neither height nor depth, nor anything else in all creation, will be able to separate us from the love of God that is in Christ Jesus our Lord. (vv. 38 and 39)

Baptism is not simply a passport to a new life in a Christian community; it implies rights and obligations as well as conferring a new status in Christ. This status is important because it unites each Christian with what called 'the first fruits' of Christ's victory over death. Paul dwells at length on the idea that

Christians have inherited a new life through Christ's victory. Jesus came as the second Adam. The first Adam was made in the image of God but through his disobedience caused the fall and introduced death into the perfect Garden of Eden. Paul argues that because of his righteousness even to the cross, Jesus frees people from the curse of Adam's disobedience and from the finality of death.

> For as in Adam all die, so in Christ all will be made alive. (1 Cor, 15:22)

Cardinal Newman set this doctrine to poetry much more eloquently than can be stated here:

> O loving wisdom of our God!
> When all was sin and shame,
> A second Adam to the fight
> And to the rescue came.
>
> O generous love! That he who smote
> In Man, for man, the foe,
> The double agony in Man,
> For man, should undergo,
>
> And in the garden secretly,
> And on the cross on high,
> Should teach his brethren, and inspire
> To suffer and to die.

> (John Henry Newman, 'Praise to the Holiest in the Height', verses 2, 4, & 5)

Later in life, Paul argued this point in much greater detail in his letter to the Romans. Here he argues that Christians are freed from sin which had had dominion over the Jews of the Old Testament, and indeed had over himself as Saul the Pharisee, but now the new community was freed from such a burden. In baptism, a different life style was open to Christians who lived in the hope of eternal life but in the meantime lived a life of love for one another and peaceable relations with those around them.

> Therefore, just as sin entered the world through one man, and death through sin, and in this way death came to all men, because all sinned— 13 for before the law was given, sin was in the world. But sin is not taken into account when there is no law. 14 Nevertheless, death reigned from the time of Adam to the time of Moses, even over those who did not sin by breaking a command, as did Adam, who was a pattern of the one to come.

> 15 But the gift is not like the trespass. For if the many died by the trespass of the one man, how much more did God's grace and the gift that came by the grace of the one man, Jesus Christ, overflow to the many! 16 Again, the gift of God is not like the result of the one man's sin: The judgment followed one sin and brought condemnation, but the gift followed many trespasses and brought justification. 17 For if, by the trespass of the one man, death reigned through that one man, how much more will those who receive God's abundant provision of grace and of the gift of righteousness reign in life through the one man, Jesus Christ. (Romans 5:12–17)

The point about any revolutionary doctrine is that it can be misinterpreted by people of lesser judgment. Paul is arguing that law was inaugurated in order to guide people who were of Adam's stock and thus required law to guide acceptable behaviour. Christians were free from the law insofar as the risen Jesus had restored the potential for righteousness and had, to use Bultmann's phrase, been 'right-wised' before God. This new word is in fact in place of justification before God, which had been offered to all who believed and were baptized. However, this doctrine had one fatal weakness that Paul was quick to recognise. If people were free from sin and from the law, could they not do as they pleased? Paul had to warn them against the attitude, 'eat, drink and be merry for tomorrow you may die'.

Paul had two choices in the way he could warn the early Christians: he could legislate for their behaviour; or he could remind them that they had inherited a spiritual body in baptism. It is at this point that we begin to see the emergence of a community that was obligated to be inclusive and caring in new ways, some of which were shown in the last chapter. Paul chose to encourage those to whom he wrote to imitate Christ. Some may have had knowledge of Jesus' life; others had garnered stories about him that they could apply in their own situations. There is evidence that Paul consciously did this in many of his letters. In Romans he spoke sternly about a 'couldn't care less attitude' whilst in 1 Corinthians he contrasted the Corinthians divisive behaviour by saying, 'And now I will show you the most excellent way'. (1 Corinthians 12:31b) Paul then writes the more beautiful of two hymns in his letters about love and the imitation of Christ. The second hymn is even more pertinent in this argument because it makes very clear how people are to behave if they have any hope of aspiring to Christ's humility and obedience in Philippians 2:6–11:

> Your attitude should be the same as that of Christ Jesus:
> 6 Who, being in very nature God,
> did not consider equality with God something to be grasped,
> 7 but made himself nothing,
> taking the very nature of a servant,
> being made in human likeness.
> 8 And being found in appearance as a man,
> he humbled himself
> and became obedient to death—
> even death on a cross!
> 9 Therefore God exalted him to the highest place
> and gave him the name that is above every name,
> 10 that at the name of Jesus every knee should bow,
> in heaven and on earth and under the earth,
> 11 and every tongue confess that Jesus Christ is Lord,
> to the glory of God the Father.

Jesus offered an example of unconditional acceptance of all who came to him. He performed healing miracles without question and taught without condemnation. He allowed his antagonists to condemn themselves out of their own mouths instead. He offered the vision of a society where the poor were blest, not because they were poor, but because they had less to lose than the rich man who wished to follow him. This is all recorded in the Gospels that were known but similar sentiments and notions would have been available orally to the early Christians as well. The genius of Paul lay not in legislating for his new communities but by offering them a new image of what a Christian community might look like and how it would automatically sustain mutual respect and tolerance for all who sought to be part of it. In other words, he showed a way in which the Galatian text could be implemented in daily living.

Body of Christ

The Body of Christ is first and foremost a social body which is organic in nature. No one is indispensable and it is impossible to be selective once someone has been accepted into membership. J. A. T. Robinson comes close to a holistic theory of the Church when he states, whilst commenting on 1 Corinthians 12: 12, that 'The unity of Christ, as of the human body, is his [Paul's] starting point'. He then proceeds to show that the body cannot in fact consist only of 'one member', but must be 'many'... The point of the verses that follow... is not that the different members must be united among themselves... but precisely that there must be more than one member if there is to be a body at all. 'We are not members of the Church, as we might be of a trade union; but are members in the unity of the Body of Christ which is the Church'. (Robinson, 1951: p 59) His latter remark underlines the fact that the body is a spiritual one not a legal enterprise. Paul never wrote a constitution for his communities! An individual Christian without the body is cut off from the richness of living in community. She cannot share, in fact, in Christian faith devoid of the sacrament of the Eucharist, which is the reminder of the body of Christ.

The eucharist can only be celebrated in fellowship and this is understood in many circles by the anglicized Greek word, *koinonia*. Koinonia implies the action together of likeminded people meeting in trust, equality and united by a common cause. The church, or early

Christian communities, represented bodies exemplifying the qualities of unity. The modern ecumenical movement always equates koinonia with the celebration of the eucharist and laments the churches inability to unite around this gift from Christ to his community. Most of the letters of Paul deal with fellowship and mutual trust to a greater or larger extent and N. T. Wright describes the process of koinonia in Philemon as '... the idea of 'interchange,' that mutuality of Christian living which, arising from common participation in the body of Christ, extends beyond mere common concern into actual exchange'. (Wright, 1991; p 51) What is suggested by this and other commentators' understanding of the early community is that people acted not out of self-interest but a common interest that included all. When it comes to a discussion of the nature of communion, a Lambeth Conference report suggests that koinonia should be translated as 'holding something in common' and that the act of communion is the symbolic celebration of our common faith. (Lambeth Conference, 1998; §14)

> Koinonia also defines the relationship between humankind and God. It is reflected on the human level as love understood as solidarity "From one ancestor, he has made all nations to inhabit the whole earth" (Acts 17:26), and it issues in relationships of respect and justice "Those who do not love a brother or sister whom they have seen, cannot love God whom they have not seen" (1 John 4:20). (*ibid*, §15)

The purpose of the subsequent chapters in this section is to examine whether the lofty expectations of the church are met in the inclusion of people with disabilities.

Paul uses the human body throughout to illustrate what he means by the Body of Christ. He does so, conscious that our bodies are the closest experience we have to understanding total dependency of one member upon another. We understand the pain of losing a part and we can imagine the value that each part has to us. It is an ingenious vehicle of illustration.

> 14 Now the body is not made up of one part but of many. 15 If the foot should say, "Because I am not a hand, I do not belong to the

body", it would not for that reason cease to be part of the body. 16 And if the ear should say, "Because I am not an eye, I do not belong to the body", it would not for that reason cease to be part of the body. 17 If the whole body were an eye, where would the sense of hearing be? If the whole body were an ear, where would the sense of smell be? 18 But in fact God has arranged the parts in the body, every one of them, just as he wanted them to be. 19 If they were all one part, where would the body be? 20 As it is, there are many parts, but one body.

21 The eye cannot say to the hand, "I don't need you!" And the head cannot say to the feet, "I don't need you!" (1 Corinthians 12:14–21)

It is part of being human to experience fear of loss – loss of an organ, a limb or life itself, which is not shared with the animal kingdom whose members do not anticipate loss or have any conception of danger except by flight. Paul is suggesting that we must love all parts of the Body of Christ, the people to whom we are united in spiritual fellowship as much as we love our own bodies.

The next thing we must learn to respect is function. Many people have a very low regard for parts of the body and are ashamed of them. Paul suggests that we must treat such organs with modesty but regard their function as important. There is not one part of the human body that can readily be lost without causing loss of function in other parts. Similarly, we must begin to appreciate those who are in fellowship with Christ. Thus, he continues to write:

… those parts of the body that seem to be weaker are indispensable, 23 and the parts that we think are less honourable we treat with special honour. And the parts that are unpresentable are treated with special modesty, 24 while our presentable parts need no special treatment. But God has combined the members of the body and has given greater honour to the parts that lacked it, 25 so that there should be no division in the body, but that its parts should have equal concern for each other. 26 If one part suffers, every part suffers with it; if one part is honoured, every part rejoices with it. (1 Corinthians 12:22–25)

Paul uses the word 'honour' four times in these last verses, which leaves little doubt that every part of the body and function must be respected. He does in fact offer a list of special functions in the next verses but he does so because the reality of the Church is that certain functions are going to be more important just as the head, as the centre of our senses, is manifestly more important to the body.

> 27 Now you are the body of Christ, and each one of you is a part of it. 28 And in the church God has appointed first of all apostles, second prophets, third teachers, then workers of miracles, also those having gifts of healing, those able to help others, those with gifts of administration, and those speaking in different kinds of tongues. 29 Are all apostles? Are all prophets? Are all teachers? Do all work miracles? 30 Do all have gifts of healing? Do all speak in tongues? Do all interpret? 31 But eagerly desire the greater gifts.

The model, which Paul has given us, does not work so well in a society that is constantly conscious of status. Paul demands that we respect all members but our modern minds prefer to put people into hierarchies and to measure everything by the importance of its function and we are probably more obsessed by the need, or even lack of, modesty surrounding our sexual organs than at the time when Paul wrote. As the second part will show, we now devalue anyone who cannot fulfil a useful function and we measure success by the extent of one's contribution towards society. Paul's talk of weakness, both in his model and when referring to his 'thorn in the flesh', has become dangerously misunderstood in today's parlance. Modern theologians have become aware of the 'weakness' of disabled people and have equated respect with support and aid. Margaret Thatcher was recalled by the late David Sheppard as saying, 'compassion is so condescending' (Obituary in the *Observer* on 6th March, 2005), and many people with disabilities might agree with her in a very qualified sense that they do not need compassion because it underlines the feeling that they are weak. Paul used the term 'weak' in the context of a society, which was unused to having disabled priests or religious teachers, and where he personally felt the pressure of his illness or impairment as he fought hard to teach. Many pastors today often feel guilty when they are ill and must neglect their pastoral duties. It is unfortunate that this meaning has been taken out of its historical context and applied to the Body of Christ today. The word 'weak' is used by Paul twenty-seven times in his letters. It has negative connotations as for instance in most of the criticisms of those who live without grace. There is however, another negativity when Paul actually uses the word positively to suggest qualities that engender spiritual wholeness when it is so perceived. Take, for example, 1 Corinthians 1:27:

> But God chose the foolish things of the world to shame the wise;
> God chose the weak things of the world to shame the strong.

In this instance, Paul echoes Jesus' words about the wise and the foolish and suggests that there is a great strength in an unworldly weakness. He also uses the term to refer to his 'thorn in the flesh', suggesting that his strength comes from his absolute dependence upon God and those around him when he is weakened by his affliction. It is not surprising therefore, that theologians have used weakness as a positive virtue and have seen special blessings in the weakness of disabled members of the Body of Christ. Verse 22 of 1 Corinthians 12 states that we must honour those parts of the body that are weak and this has generally been assumed to represent disabled people. The only problem is that Paul does not say this and that at no point implies that he is talking particularly of disabled people. There are several other interpretations of weakness in this context but the most compelling must be that some people's faith is not as strong as others' yet the whole body has a responsibility to carry such people and build them up. It is understandable that because Paul talked about his own affliction as a weakness and used the same Greek root to describe the situation that they should see a connection with disability and apply it to a general theory of the Body of Christ. It, nevertheless, remains a troublesome interpretation that will appear several times in the next chapter.

Disabled people have suffered when the word has been applied to them in a spirit of beneficence implying that they require help from the 'stronger' members of the community. This sentiment often precludes the idea that people with disabilities may have strong gifts to offer to others.

Paul only refers to the Body of Christ once in his letters as a model on which to build a Christian community. He also mentions the body in Romans and in Ephesians but not in the same detail. He does, however, speak of remembering the Body of Christ in 1 Corinthians when he writes about the Eucharist. Is the act of remembrance a remembrance of the death of Jesus – a morbid recollection – or does it imply more? Jesus probably had in mind his impending death at the time of the Last Supper and no better illustration was available than broken bread and shared wine. Paul is, however, generally credited with instituting the Eucharist and giving the act of Jesus a liturgical structure and purpose. In this act of remembrance, the death of Jesus is remembered but at the same time it is implied that we have all become part of the body and we have been taught that in baptism we share in death and rising of Christ as we experience the immersion, the going down, and the rising, the gasping for breath again as we take on the new life in Christ. So we begin to understand that we are celebrating the entire Body of Christ, the body of all who have been baptized, as we eat around the Lord's Table. This act is much more inclusive when it is understood that the body is being remembered in two ways and that no one can be distinguished at this moment of remembrance. Paul however confuses the issue as indeed this community in Corinth did. Paul obviously does not regard the Eucharist as an ordinary meal where over indulgence is acceptable. This is precisely what Corinthians did; they allowed the meal to become not only a celebration but a meal to be enjoyed to excess. The result is that Paul encourages them to come to the celebration sober and with due consideration of its purposes. Many theologians have assumed that people must have a complete understanding of what they are about to participate in prior to coming before the congregation of God's people gathered around the table. Roman Catholics have long insisted that people attend confession prior to the Mass whilst Protestants have certainly looked for understanding but have also made people prepare and examine themselves prior to the celebration. Again, in the next chapter, we shall see that the intellectual demands of the sacrament have prevented many from participation in both the past and present.

Inclusion of everyone and all activities of the church, or of society for that matter, is a utopian dream but there are certain imperatives that should guide our attitudes to inclusion. The most important is that we must respect that certain characteristics are 'given' like race and disability and because of this the obligation to include such groups becomes imperative.

Chapter Four

The Workings of the Body

St Paul liked using metaphors from biology. He explained the resurrection by considering the progress of a seed through germination to full bloom in 1st Corinthians chapter 12. His understanding of botany in this case was simple and was in fact incorrect by today's knowledge, but it is a very good illustration. In chapter 11, he develops his main metaphor about the human body comparing it to the Body of Christ. He explains that just as every organ has a function in the body, so every member of the church has a contribution and role to make within the community, which he calls the Body of Christ.

The ingenious feature of comparing the human body to that of the Body of Christ lies in the recognition that it is an organic body in which every part depends on each other for its survival and growth. There is a grace and economy in the design of the body, which compels us to believe that every part has a value and function which is intrinsic to the successful functioning of the whole body. Whilst some organs like the heart may seem to be of outstanding importance, it is no less important than the innermost parts of our bowels or any other small organ. Paul however seems to accord greater importance to some parts than other organs. This may be due to beliefs in his time of a different morphology of the body and a heightened sense of modesty which relegated certain organs to our subsidiary role. Paul probably conceived of the body in terms of contemporary images of the body, which may have been very different from our mechanistic or organic understanding today. The body was divided into zones each with different functions and were determinant of different emotions. It would be perfectly understandable to expect Paul to demand the utmost modesty surrounding our sexual organs and it is known that Jesus may well have looked to a threefold zoning of the human body when it came to defining miracles. Pilch outlines three such zones that stressed different levels of importance to our way of thinking today:

1) The emotional and thinking zone
2) The communication zone and
3) The zone which controls our ability to carry out 'purposeful action'

These zones are represented by heart-eyes, mouth-ears, and hands-feet respectively. (Pilch, 2000; p107) All three focus on function and may inevitably have lead to a subjective hierarchy of preferred functions. Whatever his beliefs were, it led him to offer the opinion that certain weaker organs were dependent on the stronger:

> ... those parts of the body that seem to be weaker are indispensable, 23 and the parts that we think are less honourable we treat with special honour. And the parts that are unpresentable are treated with special modesty, (1 Corinthians 12:22–23

The weaker parts are indispensable and their function is not to be doubted; but it is the nature of this function that will occupy a large part of this chapter. This is because when functions are translated into members of the Body of Christ, the temptation to recognize that some members are weaker has become a major obstacle in the modern search for inclusive ecclesiology. Many groups have latched on to the word 'weak' and used it to promote a theology which does not fully recognize the function which Paul really ascribed to the weaker organs. Paul was not thinking of disabled people when he wrote this although he was minded to remember his own weakness when he was ill and how this created a willingness around him on the part of members of the church to support him. In a sense, he gave to his weakness a function – a function of eliciting help and so bringing a glory to God in the actions of other people's care. Such a function served two purposes, neither of which is fully acceptable today. Firstly, it gave an extra purpose to those who could offer help to others; and secondly, it reminded the church of its obligations to the weaker members who ever they may be. The former sanctioned a charitable approach; the latter, assumed permission to talk about and for people with disabilities.

In recent literature, there has been a tendency to consider that disabled people were the weaker members. There is only one positive aspect of such a belief and that is the recognition that their function as part of the church is vital irrespective of their strength. However, thereafter all observations must be negative. The simplest observation is that disabled people neither regard themselves as weak nor are in fact weak. They have rebelled against the negativity of the word 'disabled' and have tried many devices to make it sound positive. Some churches refer to 'differently abled' people or write the word 'disabled' thus: disABLED. The majority have worked hard to put simply a certain pride in the word 'disabled' itself. If it is to be used with pride as a label, it must always refer to people – disabled people – and it must be seen to be nothing other than part of an adjectival phrase. They eschew 'the disabled' and prefer to acknowledge that disability is a process by which people find themselves unable to carry out certain functions because of the barriers erected by society. The examples are numerous but take as an example the inability to enter a building because of steps, which may lack either a ramp or a handrail or both. If there is to remain a negative connotation in weakness, it must be made redundant by more positive images of the role that people with disabilities play in the Body of Christ.

There are, therefore, two distinct views that arise out of the interpretation of Paul's comments on weakness when it comes to disability. The first is put about by people who talk about disabled people rather than for them and who find their gifts in what they inspire within themselves. The second view of disability is by people who have personal experience of it and talk as people with disabilities or who are deeply involved with them as carers and loved ones. For them the gift that people with disabilities can offer becomes a gift, which is intrinsic to them, and emerges as their involvement in the Body of Christ and, indeed, in love grows. These two approaches both challenge the church but do so in different ways. Both approaches demand a response but the first one, that of talking about disabled people, does not build any dynamic into the lives of people with disabilities but gives life to those who are for them; whereas the second approach offers life to all. It will be plainly obvious that this book favours the second approach and finds it difficult to sympathize with the first. Frankly, the first approach is condescending, the second can be liberating. The first is pietistic, the second liberating. The first is expressive of well-intentioned Roman Catholic writers but is also expressed by Protestants such as Hauerwas and other groups like Prospects. The main corpus of writing comes from L'Arche community and as we shall see later tends to be expressive of a charitable model of disability. Such a model always tends to objectify those who are receiving the love or charity whereas the alternative approach makes the internal qualities of people shine forth on their own merit. It is to Hauerwas and L'Arche in America that our attention must focus. I think that I must justify what follows by expressing my deep depression when people with disabilities appear to be objectivized. Such people are very necessarily giving voice to the voiceless; but the special nature of that voice demands exactingly critical standards. If the reader can wait for a synthesis, balance will hopefully be restored.

Stanley Hauerwas is a Southern Baptist from Texas who is a Professor at Duke University in North Carolina and now a United Methodist. He first encountered 'retarded' adults when he visited an institution as a student. He does not claim to have an intimate knowledge of people with learning difficulties now but he is still invited to address the matter. He is a pacifist, which is only relevant in passing, who finds mentally 'handicapped' people attractive precisely because they do not have the malice and intrigue which characterises the politicians whom he would characterize as 'warmongers'. This recent book, which is edited by John Swinton and entitled *Critical Reflections of Stanley Hauerwas' Theology of Disability,* compiles much of Hauerwas' understanding of the theology of disability in an accessible way. It combines a comprehensive collection of his work with commentaries or dialogues by other experts in the field in an interesting and readable format and dismisses pessimistic and defeatist attitudes which have in the past condemned 'the retarded' to institutionalized lives. The result is a fascinating journey through the ethics of writing about and for people with learning difficulties ('the retarded'). It questions how we should best offer them dignity and a place in our midst. Much of what Hauerwas writes is aimed at parents, and addresses the problems of bringing up children with such difficulties.

Stanley Hauerwas raises questions about personhood and the nature of care. He challenges the Churches to accept the 'mentally handicapped' and to understand the true meaning of 'weakness' in the way Christians should accept society's most vulnerable into a community which displays values which are more compassionate and inclusive than society as a whole. A number of friendly critics raise issues around the ethics of writing about disability and challenge Hauerwas to develop an understanding of what it means to give disabled people independence in community homes and the opportunity to develop their own identities. By careful editing Swinton makes painful and challenging reading to a disabled person with a voice who can so readily forget the voiceless.

The book simmers with tension between those who doubt the value of 'talking about' the 'retarded' and Hauerwas' rather old fashioned stance. Retarded has been the name given to people with learning difficulties in America for a long time, only to be succeeded by 'mentally handicapped' but now the independent living movement are beginning to persuade people that neither are appropriate terms. In reaction to Hauerwas' use of 'retarded', John O'Brien quotes a man with learning difficulties;

> The quotation marks surrounding "the retarded" are not a postmodern gesture but the fruit of counsel offered by my friend, Peter Park, who has lived his whole life with the consequences of being understood and treated in terms of the label, including spending 18 years in an institution for "the retarded" after his parents followed professional advice to place him there. Peter abhors the word as an enemy of the kinds of relationships that he and I believe are fundamental signs that the Spirit is at work slowly building a decent and diverse community. "Retarded," Peter

advised, "was the excuse for putting us in institutions, for sterilizing us, for keeping us without any real work to do, for putting us in time-out cells and restraints, because we didn't do what staff told us quick enough to suit them.

(O'Brien, in Swinton, 2004; p 46f)

In this volume of articles and debate, the rights of disabled people are an important issue, which surfaces at various points throughout the book. Hauerwas is often concerned to write about children and this raises yet another difficulty, namely, that people with learning difficulties are often talked of as children or admired for their child-like qualities, neither of which add to the struggle for independence. To his credit, Hauerwas does describe himself as an outsider but tends to address an audience of parents and to extol the virtues and undoubted gifts which they have developed as parents of disabled children. These parents become adept at advocating for their children at all levels of society and politics and, according to Hauerwas, they show a remarkable willingness to challenge the medical profession in order to gain the best they can for their children. The point that seems to be missed is that Hauerwas is giving to those who are 'retarded' a function which is dubious in the extreme. The function he seems to offer is that of inspiring or prodding others to work on their behalf. It is the issue of pacifism, which was mentioned above, writ into all aspects of life. It is indeed a prompts Michael Bérubé to write:

> ... the recognition of our fellow humans as fellow humans depends not on our innate, species-specific qualities or our status as creatures of the divine will, but on quotidian, sublunary forms of political deliberation that make "recognition" of one's humanity a matter of embodied social policy. It is therefore all the more urgent, on my account, that persons with mental retardation be represented in the public square when they cannot represent themselves; and it is all the more urgent that persons with mental retardation who have long been presumed to be constitutively unable to represent themselves be granted the material means to represent themselves as best they can.

(Bérubé, in Swinton, 2004; p 33)

If a gift or a function is to be ascribed to an organ in the body of Christ, it must be a gift that is intrinsic to the subject and not an objectified function which is ascribed by someone else and used by someone else. Such a move is alienating and frankly makes depressing and boring reading. The interest in this book about Hauerwas is that these issues are tackled and a corrective offered. The issue illustrates how inclusion can often be achieved without involving those who most need to be included. There can be nothing more inclusive than a gathering of anxious parents or an interested church committee in people with learning difficulties but if they include them only by talking of them, it is not true inclusion.

The second function that has to be questioned is the charitable function which suggests that people are inspired by their need to help others to become included. L'Arche often falls into this trap by assuming that you can talk about the gift of charity as if it is tackling the problem of inclusion when, in fact, it may only be tackling the needs of those who serve people with disabilities. It finds attractiveness in such inclusion which offers so much intellectual gain to those who offer the charity but to those who receive it, only a vastly improved quality of life.

Thus far, one man's quest to help and include people with learning difficulties has been considered. Now our focus turns to L'Arche which was founded by a French Canadian academic in 1964 when he discovered and befriended two disabled men who had been institutionalized for many years. He took them into his home and from this small beginning founded an international movement which offers community homes to disabled people throughout the world. L'Arche is predominately Roman Catholic although it professes no denomination and accepts all people as members and helpers. In founding the community, Jean Vanier wished to live out the preaching of Jesus and drew particular attention to the Beatitudes. To this latter, the centrality of the Magnificat and the Footwashing might be added. At the centre of L'Arche's Charter is a quest for unity of humanity drawn together by mutual care and respect and the idea that their communities should reflect the body of Christ is never far from the surface of the document. The fourth of five fundamental principles enshrined in the charter reads:

> Weakness and vulnerability in a person, far from being an obstacle to union with God, can foster it. It is often through weakness, recognised and accepted, that the liberating love of God is revealed

The other principles affirm the rights of every individual to dignity, comfort safe and secure housing and the right to have their wishes respected. In this sense, they are not very different from current legislation in the Scottish Parliament from the *Adults with Incapacities Act* through to the current consideration of legislation to protect vulnerable adults. The difference, however, is that L'Arche's principle seeks to protect such adults from creeping elective abortion and euthanasia.

Involvement with L'Arche has proved attractive to many theologians besides Jean Vanier. He himself makes much of the healing of communities and reminds us that at the end of the charter a concern is expressed for all who are oppressed by being cast out and neglected by an acquisitive society which is only concerned with perfection. He is concerned with the brokenness of all, and has written movingly of the exclusion of so many. Vanier grounds brokenness in the Fall but identifies mankind's suffering in the rejection by society of so many who are socially disadvantaged or unacceptable.

> Our God is a God of life and light.
> When God creates, it is life and light that is given.
> To understand the depth of our brokenness
> we need to look at the wholeness in which we were created,
> a wholeness that comes from total communion with God.
> (Vanier, 1988; p 17)

Other theologians like Nouwen have stressed how important it is to greet the stranger into the household of God when we are often so afraid and appalled by their presence. He writes of the beauty of caring for and accepting profoundly disabled people and offers a theology based upon their acceptance and understanding the effect their presence has upon you as 'the helper becomes the helped'. (Nouwen, 1986)

This discussion highlights two issues. First, despite the manifest good L'Arche does and the many lives that have been improved beyond recognition outwith the institutions that they might expect to be in otherwise. There is still a deep desire to talk of 'the weak' and to illustrate how rewarding caring for them can be and how insightful the experience can be for those who have not encountered people with disabilities before. Yet, in many ways, what L'Arche offers is a Christian version of care in the community. Many of their aims have been achieved in secular society with carers who have shown the same qualities of tenderness and devotion but without the need to put a Christian gloss on the reasons why they are inspired to work selflessly for their clients. Second, L'Arche must be challenged to rid itself of this obsession with the weak and to develop neutral language that is reflected in modern legislation dealing with secular care in the community.

This is not to suggest that the entire religious community is wrong in the way it addresses encounters with people with disabilities. Frances Young points out that the Roman Catholic Church has always had a tendency to adopt a charitable model towards the disabled and to over-sentimentalize their encounters with disabled people:

> There is a long-standing tradition in Catholic piety of discerning the image of God not in the rich and powerful but rather in the poor. This has motivated charitable works, and has been seen as fulfilling most directly the demands of the Gospel. These days liberation theology claims that tradition, taking the option for the poor, but it also offers a critique: charity can be patronising, it can trap the poor in their poverty.

(Frances Young, unpublished paper presented in December, 2000)

She stands with writers like Swinton who have developed a more inclusive language that adequately expresses Christian concern for the inclusion of people with disabilities in the body of Christ. Young's point is well illustrated by statements made by Pope John Paul II in his Jubilee Message on Sunday, 3rd December, 2000:

> "Blessed are the poor in spirit, those who mourn, those who are persecuted for righteousness' sake", for great will be their reward in heaven! This is the paradox of Christian hope: *what seems humanly a ruin, is in the divine plan always a plan of salvation.* Let us depart encouraged by this Jubilee day, one entirely marked by the Gospel Beatitudes. Christ, our travelling companion, is our joy. In a few days' time, we will contemplate him in the mystery of his birth: from Bethlehem, where he chose to make himself one of us, he will renew his message of happiness. [Italics original]

(http://www.vatican.va/holy_father/john_paul_ii/speeches/docume
nts/hf_jp-ii_spe_20001203_jubildisabled_en.html)

His statement, which is well intentioned, objectifies disabled people by making them objects of Christian pity and charity. These characteristics, in turn, feed a justification for inclusion in the body of Christ, which can be outdated and patronizing. If people with learning difficulties must be talked about, it must be in such a way that the body remains free to accept them with no strings attached to their purpose or being. It is simply in being that they have the right to exist within the body and to receive the sacraments of baptism and of holy communion because of their understanding which may be different from ours but is still hidden deep within their being.

The attractiveness of living in a community, which has a family ethos and a commitment to inclusion, is indeed attractive. To be able to affirm that you are accepted as a disabled person who is valued beyond the ifs and buts of euthanasia and abortion can be even more comforting for anxious parents and carers as well as aware people with disabilities. L'Arche offers inclusion with single-mindedness of purpose which secular community care can never offer and which is never offered in many of the countries in which the movement operates.

There is a deep sense in which people with disabilities are always going to be spoken of and for by articulate members of L'Arche, but there are articulate members who are relatives and carers of profoundly disabled people. Frances Young is one such mother of Archie who has learning difficulties and has suffered from increasing problems from his physical disabilities. Frances Young is a Professor of Theology at the University of Birmingham and knows how difficult it is to write of the reality of caring for someone, who is so demanding, yet who can evince so many gifts. One of her most moving chapters is based upon a lecture given at the university and entitled, 'The Crooked Timber of Humanity'. She was criticized by students for using such a politically incorrect title but she persisted because it described the frailty of living with and loving such a profoundly disabled person with so many distressing illnesses. (Young, 1990) She is capable of powerfully describing the gifts that can be found in every person by drawing on her work on 2 Corinthians. She makes use of a text from 1 Corinthians 4:7:

> But we have this treasure in jars [vessels] of clay to show that this all-surpassing power is from God and not from us.

Clay is such a powerful material in the Bible. We are created from dust and God is often figured as a potter moulding us, as He will. Moreover, here we have the important treasure of faith and of understanding being stored in an unprepossessing vessel of clay. Young argues that it is as if untold gifts are hidden in the bodies of such disabled people ready to be released and perceived when the vessel is broken; or allowed to display its contents in the relationships we can build with disabled people. She writes:

> And this is where L'Arche comes in. Because we have perceived beauty in damaged bodies, treasure in vulnerable and fragile persons. I share the L'Arche experience every night when I feed my severely disabled son and prepare his twisted and impaired body for bed. In the everydayness of attending to bodily functions, eating and defecating, washing and dressing, touching and caressing, the sanctity of bodies is acknowledged, and the presence of treasure within brokenness.

(Young, unpublished paper, *circa* 2002)

This quotation contains all the references which will be found in quotations in the next chapter, but there is a sense here that Young is talking about God given gifts not about their perception and certainly within the context of the bond of kinship and blood. Nothing is objectified but rather the gift is brought out and described for all who are willing to see and is offered as part of the community, which is L'Arche. The gift of the individual organ within the body of Christ does not have to be described in terms of its function but rather in terms of its existence and existential effect on others.

Now that last sentence is getting dangerously close to the position that had previously been criticized. Michael Bérubé argues, also as a parent of a son with Down syndrome, that we must be careful how, if at all, we should justify the existence of people with such disabilities.

> It's something like the belief that people with Down syndrome were "put" here to humanize the rest of us. It's nice enough if this actually happens, since there are few among us who would not benefit by being more compassionate, but as a general principle it becomes less attractive the longer you look at it. I mean, personally, I hope none of us was put here for the benefit of others.

(Bérubé, 1996; p 238)

Michael Bérubé wrote these remarks at the end of a long discussion of altruism and was attempting to temper the duties we have to people with learning disabilities to our obligations to help them to meet their own needs and aspirations, all be they limited. He surveys the arguments against altruism which are displayed by evolutionary 'fundamentalists' like Richard Dawkins in *The Selfish Gene* (1976) who argue that the evolutionary process excludes altruism as the 'selfish gene' seeks to dominate the survival of the fittest species. Bérubé argues that man has always sought to control his evolutionary instincts and the human aggression, which we plough so successfully into war, by an altruism which is most succinctly expressed in the 'Golden Rule'. We shall consider Jesus shortly, but the most eloquent statement of this rule came from Kant who has inspired many people to a higher duty ever since. There are several ways of expressing his formulation in his *Groundwork of the Metaphysic of Morals*:

> Act only on that maxim whereby thou canst at the same time will that it should become a universal law.

Any person who conscientiously tries to apply this rule must develop not only a love for the truth but compassion in the treatment of all, particularly human beings who are vulnerable in the extreme. Since the maxim is secular, all may follow it but, of course, Jesus gave it religious significance when he propounded his great commandment which we often disassociate from its first that gives it a religious significance and places an obligation on all who believe to show kindness and goodness to those to whom we have an obligation of care.

> 'Love the Lord your God with all your heart and with all your soul and with all your mind.' 38 This is the first and greatest commandment. 39 And the second is like it: 'Love your neighbour as yourself.' 40 All the Law and the Prophets hang on these two commandments." (Matthew 22:37–40)

The obligation upon Christians to help all their neighbours becomes an imperative as soon as Jesus' commandment guides the actions of one's heart but it is the nature of the help that is important. Bérubé's comment becomes both a challenging and poignant antidote to the enthusiastic embrace of Kantian duty by Hauerwas and by many who support L'Arche. The question must be asked whether God in His infinite wisdom does cause disability to make us better people whether we are challenged by his golden rule given through the mouth of Jesus? My answer has consistently been that God does not cause disability but that through the natural process of disability, he allows people to develop gifts which they might not otherwise have. To believe that God consciously places disability in the world is to portray a cruel and unfeeling God whose Son could not possibly have spoken of love as eloquently as he did. Where Christians respond to disability as purely a problem requiring charity, they respond to a wrong ideal of disabled people. They respond to the gifts that they receive from being in the company of disabled people rather than responding to the need to allow the innate gift of people with disabilities to develop in their own right. Bérubé suggests in his comments on Hauerwas were almost throw away remarks but in fact they go to the core of the obligations we have towards people with learning difficulties or any kind of disability.

Prospects is a large evangelical and protestant organisation for people with learning difficulties and their carers. Its website says that last year's budget was £7.5m. This is quite a turnover for an organisation which was founded by one of the editors of the Evangelical Times in 1973. Like L'Arche it was founded because people encountered disabled people indeed within the community. Their object was to establish safe homes for them at times when the carers, usually parents, were under increased strain of age and ability to care for their loved ones. The vast majority of the budget which is now expended goes on community care, in providing homes where people with learning disabilities can live independently. The charity has as its mission statement:

> PROSPECTS is a Christian voluntary organisation which values and supports people with learning disabilities so that they live their lives to the full.

The charter affirms the fundamental worth of each person and explains this in terms of the Biblical basis of respect which has always pervaded the Old Testament but is emphasised in the New. It seeks to offer the broadest opportunities to each person within their own life and operates care and concern within the context of Christian ethics. It tries to maintain Christian standards at all times and has to debate all the major issues which confront Christians in a modern society. It is interesting that it puts the opportunity of full life in the community first before focussing on involvement in the Church.

Involvement in the Church is, however, of prime importance and Prospects has services throughout Britain and offers support for those in their care and others within the context of christian worship.

The worship which is offered is adapted to the needs of people with learning and severe disabilities. Members are involved in music making and learn to sign to the music. Scripture lessons are read in plain English and kept simple and talks are backed up by activities such as puppet making and so on. Prospects is not sacramental as L'Arche is but has developed simple orders of service for Holy Communion and builds up an understanding in the course of the worship sessions. These sessions are held within the Church but separately from mainstream worship. This could be a criticism but it does offer opportunities for the creativity which comes of offering simplified worship adapted to the needs of the congregation and to the joy of carers to see their children of all ages creating a happy atmosphere.

The contrast with L'Arche is actually not very great except that there seems to be less emphasis on the body as something that has to be cared for and more emphasis on the body as requiring welfare which can then lead to worship. Many of the same problems of objectification still exists but in a different sense. The major emphasis of Prospects is to promote welfare so that people can come to Jesus in the worship which is so vibrant in the various groups.

Two other authors are of note for the way they suggest we should understand our obligations towards disabled people, particularly those with learning difficulties. John Swinton suggests that we must show 'solicitous' care towards those with either learning difficulties or mental health problems. Often their greatest burden is that of loneliness – the loneliness of isolation and the loneliness again of silence. It is well known that disabled people watch a disproportionate amount of television and for many who have learning difficulties it is easier to communicate through the CD player with pop music than by human voice. To overcome this requires the kind of care which was offered by Christ and which has been known as solicitous since the time of Aristotle. It thinks more of the other person's needs than our own and accords with the ethics of the Petrine Letters and with much of the teaching and example of Jesus. Because such an ethic places the entire focus on the disabled person, it is potentially different from that of Hauerwas because the care itself is central. Here the body of Christ honours the individual rather than concentrating on the obligation and duties of the non-disabled person. Jennie Weiss Block offers the same kind of advice but uses the word copious – copious hosting – which is how Jesus always acted when confronted with those who needed his help and understanding. She, too, writes with experience as the sister of a disabled brother and is well aware of the example of Jesus in caring, although at times she is tempted to slip into the 'charitable' model which we have criticized as being so characteristic of Catholic piety. (Block, 2002)

This chapter has naturally focused on people with learning difficulties yet many disabled people who do not have such impairments can both feel excluded from this debate and very often exclude themselves by a mistaken perception that they do not have to be concerned about people with learning difficulties. Such people, they argue, do not fully understand the social model of disability and because of their lack of consciousness of their position as disabled people do not merit a prominent place in such arguments. This is often compounded by the feeling that they depend too much upon carers and advocates and cannot campaign on their own behalf. Such views are clearly wrong but understandable when placed in the context of the voices of marginalized people. Yet, they have a right to be heard as potential of the Body of Christ whose acceptance must be above the arguments about the support of the weakest and false hierarchical nonsense. In modern thought, and not the thought that will be explored in the next chapter, all have an equal place to play a role in the life of the Body of Christ without reference to a hierarchy. The group which struggled to produce the WCC's statement on disability, 'A Church for All and of All' had always to balance the voices of the voiceless with their own rather vociferous views. They succeeded because they always returned to equality. Equality was a characteristic of the early Church as it sought to include all who were baptized into the new body and they were aware that God had always showered his mercies equally on those who were worthy of his kindness. Jesus was even more emphatic:

> He causes his sun to rise on the evil and the good, and sends rain on the righteous and the unrighteous. (Matthew 5:45)

Jesus rams home the point by adding that it is too easy for us to love those who are like us and not others. In sum, we must accept the equality of all disabled people or betray our whole argument.

It is incorrect to use the word 'weak' to describe people who may be very strong and accepting of their disability as if the quality of weakness comes with their lot in life. There is a way of understanding weakness in a constructive and equal way. Each one of us can only make the contribution to the Kingdom and the Body of Christ of which we are capable. As imperfect sinners, none of us is capable of a perfect contribution and the strength of the contribution we make can be measured by no one but God. Therefore, the weak are not identifiable by any human measure. It was Spurgeon who said in a sermon that he was absolutely incapable of taking a paintbrush and marking all those in a congregation who had been perfectly called. Such a suggestion of equality must be applied here and was applied by the *Ecumenical Disabilities Advocates Network* (EDAN), the group who were principally responsible for the statement. They ended the section on the Body of Christ with an affirmation of God's evenhanded dealings with humankind and thus proclaimed that the divisions which often appear within disabled groups were not going to be present in their statement. Section 30 ends with a list of illustrations of the way God inevitably pulls us back to a position of equality:

> Christian theology needs to interpret the imago Dei from a Christological and soteriological (the saving work of Christ for the world) stand point, which takes us beyond the usual creationist and anthropological perspectives.

> Christian theology needs to embrace a non elitist, inclusive understanding of the Body of Christ as the paradigm for understanding the imago Dei.

> Without the full incorporation of persons who can contribute from the experience of disability, the Church falls short of the glory of God, and cannot claim to be in the image of God.

> Without the insight of those who have experience of disability, some of the most profound and distinctive elements of Christian theology are easily corrupted or lost.

Chapter Six will attempt to show how much the Reformed Church has succeeded over the centuries since the Reformation to foster equality and inclusion but first we must consider whether disabled people have been given equal access to the two central sacraments of the Church, baptism and the Lord's Supper.

Chapter Five

Symbols of Acceptance

The sacraments of baptism and of the eucharist are intensely human symbols. They represent activities which none of us can avoid and which are uniquely social. We must all wash and eat and although washing tends to be a private activity eating a meal is a major social event. Both are parts of everyone's life, so we all know what is involved and implied by these symbols. They are called symbols because, in each, something ordinary is turned into an act that is full of religious meaning and purpose. This chapter asks whether the Church has always accepted that anyone may participate in the transition from ordinary to sublimely holy. The problem is that for some, the act of washing is so special an achievement, as is feeding, that the acts constitute a small miracle without any suggestion that it is holy.

> It is clear that L'Arche has a particular experience of these basic human actions. Washing and cleaning those who cannot perform these functions for themselves are a basic part of daily life in communities. As Jean Vanier constantly stresses, washing the body, when it is broken or in pain is an essential way of caring for the person, and an essential way of expressing and communicating love (Touch is a primal form of communication).
>
> We have seen how, in its earlier history, the Church associated anointing with washing. The body was plunged into water, then all the senses were anointed. Here are forms of sacramental action which may be realized in various ways in communities where washing plays so central a part.
>
> (A. M. (Donald) Allchin in Young, 1997)

L'Arche community is essentially a community where disabled people are accepted, and are made part of the living community by the dedication and help of its volunteers. It is rightly pointed out that many disabled people require help with washing and eating in a way which makes the sacraments of baptism and communion even more poignant and vivid in such a setting. Jesus prefigured both these actions in his life. Not only was Jesus himself baptized but also he prepared an understanding of it that offered an illustration of how a Christian becomes committed to baptism. In John chapter 13, there is the famous story of how Jesus took off his outer garments, took a bowl of water and washed the feet of his disciples. The story can be recounted to bring out many factors, but here we want to concentrate upon the words of Peter who remonstrated when Jesus offered to wash his feet. His master replied:

Jesus answered, "Unless I wash you, you have no part with me."

"Then Lord," Simon Peter replied, "not just my feet but my hands and my head as well!" (John 13:8b & 9)

If ever an utterance pleaded for complete immersion in the cause of another; this is a supreme example. Just as Peter wants to identify completely with the cause of another so all who go forward for baptism should seek a similar identification with the body of Christ. Yes, the essence of the complete story remains that Jesus took the form of a servant and met the basic needs of his disciples in a supreme act of hospitality. The same type of imagery is conjured up by the story of Mary washing Jesus' feet with her tears. (Luke 7:37–39) It is thus very understandable that the act takes on such symbolism and is particularly so to those who are engaged in caring for disabled people. Washing is an immensely social event: but eating is even more so.

Again we have to look at the gospels to understand how Jesus saw eating as a significant social event. Not only did he choose to illustrate his sacrifice by breaking bread and sharing wine but also he showed it in the ways he shared meals as part of his ministry. He ate with sinners and tax collectors giving men like Zacchaeus and he paid the price for such meals in the hostile questioning of the Pharisees. (Luke 19 1–9) The miracles are similarly full of eating and feeding imagery: the feeding of the five thousand and the sharing of fish by the lake in the resurrection appearances. There are many messages contained within these stories but one must surely be that there is plenty but it must be shared.

There is a wonderful story of a man who went to hell and found that there was a banquet of food beyond his wildest dreams set before him and his compatriots. The only problem was that the spoons were over three feet long, so no one was able to eat and everyone grew miserable as the food went to waste. He was given a glimpse of heaven where they had exactly the same sumptuous banquet and eating implements, but they were helping one another. Those who participate in L'Arche are well acquainted with the need to help members of the community at mealtimes and many of the helpers have written of the meaningfulness of this experience.

> Eating together is also at the very heart of a L'Arche community. Here there is a distinction to be made which may be of some importance. Some have to be fed individually - infants, the very old when they are extremely weak, the most severely handicapped; others are able to sit at table together. Both these ways of eating need to be respected and valued. Both need to be present in our celebration of the sacrament. (A. M. (Donald) Allchin in Young, 1997)

Paul formalized the meals that Jesus ate and illustrated by giving us the form of eucharist which has been used by the Church for centuries in 1 Corinthians chapter 11.

Sometimes commentators are confused by the meaning of function when considering the body of Christ. They correctly realize that Paul is using the metaphor of the human body and that each organ has a different function but they fail to realize that a) no two similar organs have exactly the same function in any different bodies: and b) they fall into the trap of assuming that there is always an ideal function for every body. This view is typical of the Enlightenment which adopted a mechanistic view of the universe and was happy with the notion that it worked like clock-work with every part performing an exact function. In a modern economy, we have tended to treat disability as a dysfunction and sought to correct it through medicine rather than to treat the social causes of it. This approach has been called the medical model of disability as opposed to the social model of disability. It begins to betray itself in much of the thinking about disability.

Many writers put a lot of emphasis on function, or the loss of it, rather than concentrating on the gifts which disabled people can offer to others and to society. In the latter part of this section, we shall see how much more fruitful a concentration on the giftedness of disabled people is compared with an emphasis on function. Let us, therefore, begin by looking at function from three perspectives: 1) a secular point of view; 2) from the point of view people with learning difficulties; and 3) the point of view of the Christian community taking a counter stand against modern culture.

A word about 'handicap' before continuing: this word has a technical meaning that is losing credibility very rapidly but it is often used by members of the L'Arche community and by theologians like Hauerwas in a non-technical sense. This is probably due to cultural lag in cases like Hauerwas; or by members of L'Arche because it is principally a French organization in origin and francophone countries still tend to use the word in ways which would be translated differently in English. These two excuses for the use of the word are in fact pretty lame and it is to be hoped that the use of 'handicap' will disappear in the near future. It is thought to be a corruption of 'cap in hand' which is suggestive of a time when disabled people begged for their living and survival.

Returning now to the three perspectives on function, the first is perhaps most important. Disabled people, and able bodied counterparts who write on disability, have often tried to play down the negativity of the word. The Churches, notably the *World Council of Churches* (WCC) have used the phrase, 'differently abled', and although this was corrected in 2003 many churches continue to use the phrase on their websites. Its shows a distinctive embarrassment with the fact that people with disabilities are different and do lack functions which others have. The negativity is also played down by the use of words such as 'disABILITY'. This is thought to stress the ability of disabled people but in fact probably draws attention to the fact that there are things they cannot do. The bottom line is that people with disabilities know their limitations and have no reason to disguise them.

The *World Health Organisation* (WHO) equated handicap with loss of function in a document dated from 1980 and this gave the word an aura of respectability and commonsense until it was supplanted by the *International Classification of Functions* (ICF) in 2001. The document argued that it was more sensible to try to classify the function of a disabled person in order to come to an understanding of not only the medical limitations placed upon an individual but the barriers that society erected to prevent full and adequate functioning. There is always a suspicion amongst disabled people against both the WCC and the WHO because of the broad sweep with which they dealt with disabled people, but this is beginning to diminish but only very slowly.

People with disabilities dislike euphemisms that do more to salve the conscience of outsiders rather than serve the needs of those who are part of a minority. This is true of any minority grouping and is witnessed by the growth in political correct language but also in the adoption of colloquialisms such as derivatives of 'cripple' such as 'crip', 'super-crip' and 'crip-time', which refers to the extra time which people with disabilities require to do normal tasks. There is a general resentment of euphemistic language and also of language which indicates an inability to accept a disability. For instance, Leonard Kriegel writes:

> Yet living as a cripple in this city turned out to be not so much a personal as a political problem. It asked me to define what I could legitimately ask of the larger community. Is access a right or a favor granted by the city? Most people, asked to choose between my right

to enter a restaurant and the integrity of one or another landmark, would discover that the lame and halt, even if called "differently abled," pose problems they would rather ignore. The now-fashionable Chelsea in which I live wants sculpted and buffed bodies. Cripples are neither sculpted nor buffed, merely broken. Christopher Reeve as Superman was a New York fantasy. Christopher Reeve in an electric wheelchair, speaking with the aid of a computer, makes the city squirm. It's not that the city is indifferent to him but that it wants to keep its distance from his problems. Yet it brags of what it has done, is doing, and will do for cripples like him. ('Beloved Enemy: A Cripple in the Crippled City' in O'brien, 2004; p 135)

The rich language which Kriegel uses illustrates vividly how fruitless an attempt to use politically correct language to describe loss of function can be. He also introduces the idea that society finds it very difficult to cope with people whose function falls short of the modern expectation of perfection within our society.

Joel Shuman argues in *The Body of Compassion* that in modern society people tend to be measured by their productivity and that the task of medicine is to restore anyone who falls short of this expectation to an acceptable level of productivity. The body is there to be repaired by either surgery or rehabilitation so that it may meet society's expectations. He goes on:

Any condition affecting one's ability to participate in the political economy tends to be seen as in some way constituting an unacceptable difference, and hence a pathology. The rise of various types of institutional care for the aged or for those with mental retardation could be understood in this way, for example, and seen as corresponding both to the notion that these persons are not normal because they are unable to participate fully in the economy and to the notion that their abnormality requires a special institutional type of care that enables others to participate fully in that economy. (Shuman, 2003; p 40f)

Shuman continues to construct a theological model of the body which asserts that a person's being is marked by his personality and that in a baptized Christian community that body is sealed by the love of Christ. Its uniqueness, and indeed its immortality are sealed by the love of God being reflected in it at all stages of life. He escapes from the emphasis on function and builds on the notion of gift and of love. This will be developed further when we turn to the giftedness of people with disabilities.

In order to examine the third perspective we turn to the work of John Swinton and the authors of essays collected by Edward Foley. Swinton has studied spirituality amongst people with learning difficulties and others with mental health problems for some time. He raises interesting points about the nature of 'spirituality'. His central methodology insists that spirituality must embrace all religions and no religion at all. It is a state of wellbeing and contentment with the world and in his research he explores with subjects their likes, dislikes, fear and elations in the world. He asks how they react to the experience of confronting death or birth, their expectations about marriage and their appreciation of music and television. Spirituality is a holistic subject and must take into consideration the whole of a person's life. (Swinton, 2001; Chapter 1) Of course, his research may be honed in on Christianity but this is not a prerequisite. It is important in this context because many of the writers who join Foley in his volume stress the point that people with learning difficulties are able to understand the symbolism of the sacraments and therefore find meaning in them. We shall see in a moment how the Church has a history of stressing the function of communion at the expense of its myriad of meanings.

First, the sacraments should be open to anyone of a pure and clean heart.

> 3 Who may ascend the hill of the Lord?
> Who may stand in his holy place?
> 4 He who has clean hands and a pure heart,
> who does not lift up his soul to an idol
> or swear by what is false.
> 5 He will receive blessing from the Lord

and vindication from God his Saviour.
6 Such is the generation of those who seek him,
who seek your face, O God of Jacob.

Psalm 24:3–6

If we think back to Hauerwas' liking of pacifism and the non-exploitative nature of people with learning difficulties, it is not hard to take from these verses an image of the type of innocence which they bring to 'the mountain of the Lord'. Dianne Bergant argues forcibly that our liberal society of today only recognises the successful and 'complete' person and applies this to those who may worship God at the most intimate sacrament. She argues that Psalm 24 shows clearly that anyone with a willing heart and ability to understand the symbolism of the sacraments should be allowed to receive them. She would argue that people with learning difficulties have an abundance of qualities to take before God in the Church's liturgy. (Bergant in Foley, 1994; chapter 1)

Even the way this has been paraphrased by the use of the word 'ability' betrays the old tendency to demand understanding but Mary Therese Harrington shows how we must capture the understanding which is latent within the catechumens with whom she deals. She suggests that we must build up 'affectivity' around the symbols that are important to people with learning difficulties and which they must appreciate before coming to the sacraments. Again, like Swinton, she stresses the simple things that may occupy minds which are slightly more egocentric than the average adult mind. However, overcoming fear of the dark and learning to sleep on one's own can be just as important to understanding God's care as any other symbols. (Harrington in Foley, 1994; Chapter 6)

Finally, why this emphasis on symbol? As Mark Francis points out Vatican II began to stress the importance of the local symbol in any congregation's celebration and worship which was now in the vernacular and well within the understanding of all. Gone was the Scholasticism which we are about to discuss and in came the joyous response of a congregation which should have included disabled people but often did not. (Francis in Foley, 1994; Chapter 4)

There is an assumption that with function must come a conscious awareness of the full implication of an act. Jean Vanier recounts a story of a little girl which illustrates this point nicely:

> Sometime ago a little girl with a handicap made her first communion. The Eucharist was beautiful; and was followed by a little celebration with the family. At one moment the girl's uncle said to her mother: "Wasn't it beautiful? It's too bad that she did not understand anything." The little girl heard the remark and with tears in her eyes said: "Don't worry, Mummy, Jesus loves me as I am". (Jean Vanier in Young, 1997; p 12)

There is a long and profound history behind the belief that you must have a full understanding of the sacraments to be able to participate. Medieval thinking about the sacraments and the subsequent training of priests led to a tendency to regard the sacraments as something that could be understood scientifically and in such a way that they were reserved in full for the priests. The mass was said in Latin, which was unintelligible to most of the congregation, and the priest held the secrets of the consecration and the transubstantiation of the elements of bread and wine. The elements were a gift offered by Christ through the Church to the congregation who were expected to have some understanding of the values of the gifts they were about to receive and aware of the grace which they might engender. The Reformers had no less of a strict understanding of the sacraments, which they reduced to two, baptism and the Lord's Supper. The emphasis was placed upon the symbolic significance of the elements and great consideration was given to whether one was prepared to receive the bread and wine which now had no magical significance.

[28]A man ought to examine himself before he eats of the bread and drinks of the cup. (1 Corinthians 11:28)

It became a central part of the communion 'season' that people prepared themselves for the sacrament by attending a series of sermons. They examined themselves on the day of the communion service when the table was fenced, in other words, when members of the congregation were asked to consider carefully whether they were fit and had a case to present before Christ as they came into his presence around the table. I remember in 1972 my last interview prior to taking my first step towards ordination. We had to answer questions on the meaning of the sacraments based on our understanding of the appropriate articles in the *Westminster Confession of Faith*. The first clause of Article XXVII reads:

> Sacraments are holy signs and seals of the covenant of grace, immediately instituted by God, to represent Christ and His benefits; and to confirm our interest in Him: as also, to put a visible difference between those that belong unto the Church and the rest of the world; and solemnly to engage them to the service of God in Christ, according to His Word.

The text of the confession is very dense and, it has to be admitted, covers almost everything that is mentioned in this chapter but the temptation was to concentrate purely upon the meaning which was one of grace and of symbolism. The whole confession, and this article of five clauses, stresses the word of God which has to be understood in order to appreciate the sacrament. Five proof texts have been removed from the quotation – it is regarded as a major act of scholarship to understand the biblical nature of the sacraments. Just as the Catholic Church sought a metaphysical understanding of the sacraments, so the Reformers demanded an intimate knowledge of scripture. In both cases, this was probably beyond many members of the congregation and certainly those with learning difficulties. As I was to learn the search for the meaning of the sacraments gave both of them a function which confused mental ability with the symbolism contained within them.

John Yoder in *Body Politics* (1992; Chapter 2) re-examines the sacrament of Holy Communion in the light of the Biblical evidence concerning common meals. He insists that all the miracles which Jesus performed around food point towards the existence of a 'common meal' within the early Christian communities. Not only do we have the miracles of the feeding of the five thousand but we have recorded miracles of Jesus causing large catches of fish to be landed and in the resurrection appearances Jesus prepares at least one meal for his disciples at the lakeside. The only material reference in the Lord's Prayer is the petition for 'our daily bread as if eating together was extraordinarily important to early Christians. The Last Supper itself is best understood as an instance of a common meal and Paul, as was previously seen, offers strict guidelines for the sharing and eating of food in the context of the Lord's Supper which he formalises in 1 Corinthians 11:22–29.

Yoder argues that the Church has adopted a forensic attitude to communion making it less of a meal and more of a highly formalised rite which offers the 'elements' in an almost magical way as consecrated bread and wine 'set apart from all common use to this holy mystery'. The idea of a meal celebrated in common is lost in the midst of ritual.

I remember, as a young assistant minister in Glasgow, taking communion to three confused old women in a geriatric ward in the local hospital. The poor souls were probably confused by my presence as well as by the sacrament but I remember feeling guilty that in some way I had to squander the sacrament on these three ladies. My feelings were reflective of the general attitude in presbyterian and other denominations in Scotland that one must fully examine oneself before going to communion. This attitude is gradually diminishing; but still makes members of such congregations concentrate on the collective act rather than its divine properties. It is an act of remembrance; and in the function, the remembrance is completed. The controversy which arises in reading material by members of L'Arche is that there is a concentration on a special meaning of the sacrament, both to them and to other members of the community. My own experience illustrates the difference between function and meaning.

The function of the sacrament refers to two inter-related components: the ritualistic traditions which have developed and evolved within the churches throughout the centuries; and also the doctrines that have inspired them, scholastically and in the popular psyche to this day. Individuals, on the other hand, invest their emotions and creative thought in building meanings into the sacrament of Holy Communion as it engages their most intimate religious experience.

I have been ordained for thirty-one years during which time I have never lifted the cup or chalice or broken bread because I have cerebral palsy and my shaky co-ordination made such delicate movements impossible. Shortly before I retired I went to a Eucharist in an Episcopalian Church which was advertized as a radical and novel way of celebrating the sacrament. Basically, it involved standing in a circle round the communion table and sharing in the distribution. I still could neither break the bread nor lift the cup and I reflected that nothing had changed over twenty-two years in the ministry. I want to place on record the fact that I became confused between meaning and function and sacrificed the former for function.

I remember going to my first communion with my mother and father at the late age of about twenty and reflecting afterwards that the wine had hardly touched my lips as my mother lifted the cup but not quite highly enough. I commented on this later, 'it doesn't matter, Jesus got very little wine on the Cross – hardly enough to whet his lips'. Mother was impressed by this statement and said something to effect that it was a remark worthy of a true Christian. Whether because her remark made modesty conceal it or whether it was just clouded in sentimentality the remark was lost to private memory until now. So be it, but was the exposition of communion much more important than the impaired function with which it was received?

I am a presbyterian and as such celebrated communion with elders on either side of me around the Lord's Table. Generally, there would be one common cup and countless trays of individual glasses and diced bread for the congregation. All my congregations shied away from general use of a common cup. One elder on the right lifted the cup whilst I said the words of consecration whilst the other on the left broke the bread sharing it firstly with me then with the others. I recall very few discussions of this practice but a consciousness that is was not possible to transport it outwith a small circle of elders who were usually confined to one presbytery. In other words, my practice was a relatively private affair known to but a few. It was also discussed at length by the committee which was charged to decide whether I could enter the ministry and the discussion was confined only to the function. It is amazing what you can learn from the then chairman thirty years on over a dinner table! Thirty years is after all the length of time government secrets are held in private. The point is that never in these thirty years was the question of meaning radically discussed. Sure, some of the elders admitted that it was nice to have added responsibility in the celebration but that was the extent of the discussion. What was never discussed was the meaning and although my mother and I occasionally reflected on the meaning it never became a matter of public discourse.

I believe that this was a tremendous loss both to me but also to several congregations that could have benefited from the insights which I had gained. I once debated with a friend whether I should take part in the celebration of the Lord's Supper in Iona Abbey. I argued that it would be impossible to carry the basket of bread around such a large Church; she argued that I had a responsibility to offer the congregation the opportunities to see how they could share the celebration in a new way and thereby plumb the depths of its meaning. I did not proceed and meaning was lost once more. If I had the thirty years over again and had developed wiser shoulders at an earlier age would it have been possible to do it differently. Would I sympathize with the members of L'Arche who have found meaning in the sacrament of eating in a community where for many it is hard and for most impossible to serve as it potentially was for me?

There is obviously a problem between discerning the function of baptism and eucharist and its more spiritual meaning. Joel Shuman

(2003) suggests a way in which it is possible to discern how function has been imposed upon us by modern society and compares it to how meaning might be developed to give us an understanding of our responsibilities to act as members of the Body of Christ with the bonds of baptism. Such a meaning would hold us together in a community standing for collective values in a society which values individual identity above all else. His arguments should take us far beyond the difficulties I had in reconciling the two during my ministry and offer us a new way forward towards inclusion.

This brings us to the heart of the third issue that was placed on the agenda sometime ago, that of the Christian community taking a counter stand against modern culture. Shuman believes that the key to understanding our role in the church is to accept the fullness of our initiation in baptism and by becoming absolutely involved in that, we begin to understand the meaning of communion. He quotes Romans chapter 6, verse 3:

> ... you know that all of us who were baptized into Christ Jesus were baptized into his death?

To be baptized is not only a spiritual reality but as such demands of us a commitment and dedication to the community of faith as great as the declaration of Peter when he asked Jesus to wash him completely so that he might identify completely with his calling. Baptism as an initiation is not simply akin to a membership card but is the beginning of a journey into a deeper relationship with Christ and those whom he has called to serve in his church. Shuman recalls the isolation of his father at the time of his death surrounded by the barriers of modern medicine, which enshrine the individual rather than the individual *within* a loving community. When we gather around the communion table we gather as a community bringing with us our commitments, carrying our crosses of convictions which we have decided to exhibit to the world whether it wants them or not. To gather without an awareness of this purpose is to gather without our membership and obligations. If we make communion simply a memorial, we can easily come without the profundity of our lives in Christ. If, as Shuman argues, we come to truly remember and represent the body of Christ that is broken in the bread, we come both to remember both the historic body of Christ and the present body of Christ in our life together and our common witness. This represents the meaning of the eucharist in a vibrant community which knows how to care for the individual and to break the barriers which are erected around the individual but are dissolved in this inclusive act of the Church.

Part Three

Reforming Attitudes

Chapter Six

Chosen, Faith and Equality

The Reformation brought with it a great democratizing movement within the Church, which has not diminished, in strength over the centuries. Everyone had equal access to Scriptures for the first time and had, in theory at least, the ability to question ministers. The reading of the Bible increased the general ability to read and it gave devout families a new gathering point in family life - worship led by the head of the household at table and at other times when the Bible could be studied.

It brought to the Calvinist Churches the end of corrupt hierarchies and introduced equality of clergy and of the Eldership. Gone were Bishops and higher offices and in came a collegiate form of government. Pastoral care was in everyone's hands and there developed a care for each other throughout the Church structures. The Church, of course, had its leading lights and an informal hierarchy was bound to develop. The equality of all was only diminished by the renewed interest in St Augustine's *City of God* and the awareness that the world was divided into those who were potential citizens and those who were not. The scholars of Geneva, Calvin, Beza and others who travelled to learn - such as John Knox - developed the idea of election which maintained that those within the Church had been elected by God from the beginning of time. We will return to this later but let us take it as read at the moment.

Faith became the source of equality within the Church. All believers were justified – justified by faith alone. The more one developed the outward signs of faith, the more one was assumed to be amongst the elect and an influence for good within the local church community.

The Reformed Church in Scotland was not noted for its involvement in social issues. The problems of housing and abject poverty were not really tackled until close to the end of the 19th century by men like Thomas Chalmers and south of the border by men who broke away from the established church of England to engage in the fight against deprivation, as did William Booth the founder of the Salvation Army for example. What the church in Scotland did establish was a parish system, which exercised a considerable degree of social control, and which primarily looked after public and private morality, educated young people, and offered a degree of stability when people moved from one area to another. (Devine, 1999)

Many people abused the potential for equality which they ought to have espoused in the church and reached out 'far above their station'. Such Elders and members were satirized in Robert Burns' poem, 'Holy Willie's prayer':

> O Thou, who in the heavens does dwell,
> Who, as it pleases best Thysel',
> Sends ane to heaven an' ten to hell,
> A' for Thy glory,
> And no for ony gude or ill
> They've done afore Thee!

The poem also reflects the deep psychological tension under which the thoughtful churchperson lived when s/he contemplated the doctrine of predestination. This chapter is in fact going to look at the derived consequences of the Reformation as they affected disabled people who were not part of the process of democracy within the church and lacked the means to enter into the system. The chapter cannot look at the veracity of the doctrines but will rather look at the derived social consequences as they affected people with disabilities. As the title indicates, three areas will be examined: the doctrine of the elect; the expectation of faith and equality that never actually happened.

Whether one was chosen or not was ultimately a mystery but the mists of the mystery could be lifted by social observation. The entire Reformation seemed to centre on justification by faith and is well expressed Harink when he sets up the argument he wishes to dissolve;

> When Protestants think of Paul they think of the doctrine of justification by faith in Jesus Christ. Justification means being made right before God through faith alone in Jesus' atoning sacrifice alone, apart from the law or any other human works or striving.

(Harink, 2003; p 25)

The Reformation was nothing if it was not about St Paul. 'Gentle Jesus, meek and mild' was replaced by the severity of Paul who appeared to codify the works of Jesus as described in the Gospels into a purer doctrinal form. In this situation, the love of Christ could be easily forgotten and substituted by a forensic examination of God's mercy displayed on the cross.

The Reality of Being Chosen

Although the Reformation heralded a new democracy in the church, human nature being what it is, members of the church wanted signs that they were chosen, perhaps even signs that people merited a higher place in the pecking order of a congregation. Many regarded their work as a 'calling' and entry into a profession was a 'vocation'. 'One's vocation became simply one's work. To be sure, for the Reformers this was a wider concept than what we have come to mean by work - which is, roughly, a job for the doing of which one is paid, a way to make a living. For example, familial responsibilities, though they do not belong to the sphere of work ...' (Meilaender, 2000) It was not the fault of doctrine but of human nature. It was derived from doctrine, which neither the Reformers nor the clergy had intended, but it developed nevertheless. There were people within the church who wrote tracts which encouraged a belief in the inequality of members as regards their favour with God and they pandered to a need within the rising entrepreneurial classes. In the *Protestant Ethic and the*

Spirit of Capitalism, Max Weber showed how tracts and books by publicists and sermons by American preachers like Benjamin Franklin began to encourage this class of people to think that success at work and the development of a calling were an indication that one has been truly elected as one of the church.

> In practice this means that God helps those who help themselves. Thus the Calvinist, as it is sometimes put; himself creates his own salvation, or, as-would be more correct, the conviction of it. But this creation cannot, as in Catholicism, consist in a gradual accumulation of individual good works to one's credit, but rather in a systematic self-control which at every moment stands before the inexorable alternative, chosen or damned.

(Weber [translated by Talcott Parsons], 1958; p 115)

When this was combined with the freeing up of commercial practices surrounding usury a potent combination of beliefs came into existence; first, a desire to work hard to show one's worth, and second, a climate in which capitalism could flourish became attractive to the successful in the churches. Simple acquisition of wealth was to be disdained; its purpose was to reflect the glory of God:

> He gets nothing out of his wealth for himself, except the irrational sense of having-done his job well. But it is just that which seems to the pre-capitalistic man so incomprehensible and mysterious, so unworthy and contemptible. That anyone should be able to make it the sole purpose of his life-work, to sink into the grave weighed down with a great material load of money and goods, seems to him explicable only as the product of a perverse instinct, the *auri sacra fames*.

(Weber [translated by Talcott Parsons], 1958; p 72)

In Scotland, the high kirks or parish churches continued to serve everyone within the community. The Disruption of 1843 tended to backed by an affluent laity who had money to build churches but also the opportunity to wear the badge of success. In cities up and down the land there were churches that displayed for all to see the success of those who had responded to their calling and been rewarded by riches that were not necessarily stored in heaven but very much on this earth.

The Church with newfound democratic power could now offer that power to the privileged few. Although mention has been made of Scotland, these trends were writ large in America. It is to America that we must now turn to see whether this historical model really has any relevance to the inclusion or exclusion of disabled people. In the 1960's, Jean Russell wrote a book entitled *God's Lost Cause* (1968) which examined the way the Protestant churches of America had ignored the blacks within their congregations because they had no outward sign of calling of God. They did not conform to Puritan values of the earlier American settlers nor did they develop the advocacy that would have been necessary to show their consciousness within a church that showed the success of the whites to all who espoused the doctrines of the elect, of the chosen and of success. Russell's book was a pioneer in showing how a minority could be kept back by doctrine and even by the churches selective development of the Social Gospel which did little to improve the lot of blacks.

Is it possible to extrapolate from these sources of inequality some insight into disability. It has to be said at the outset, that at the time of the rapid expansion, churches associated with the entrepreneurial classes were not faced with a clamour of disabled people wanting to join the new growth in churches. People with disabilities were at that time institutionalized and it was better that they were not seen in public. In addition, many had very short life expectancy which meant that Victorian churches could be built with impressive pseudo-Gothic frontages full of steps and ornate nooks and crannies saying more about status then people. However, what the prevailing ethos in the church did was to make it quite acceptable to ignore those who showed a lesser calling than the successful. People who were deprived of educational opportunity and life-chances in general were likely to be ignored in the equality stakes, which the doctrine of the church advocated, but human nature fought against.

All this was the first sign that the democracy of the Reformation has failed and that the equality, which was enshrined in the American constitution, was conferred selectively as that constitution was interpreted by religious voices rather than the secular influences which might have been behind its ringing tones of equality. It has taken until the latter half of the twentieth century to build up a head of steam for a campaign to offer equality to all minorities. Lack of opportunity and of education gave disabled people no opportunity to show any hidden talents that they might have. They did not have access to any of the career structures which marked the successful Christian and were hardly available to women in the century prior to the twentieth. People with disabilities were only accommodated into the life of the church as objects of charity and many institutions were inspired or even founded by established churches. For those who promoted such charitable deeds, their careers became objects of admiration and role models that once again showed the true nature of a Christian calling. The calling was to professional carers not to disabled people themselves. The tradition has persisted to this day but now disabled people have the opportunities, education and the capacities to pursue their own careers and to fulfil their own 'callings' in many much respected spheres of life.

Nevertheless, just as we can paint a broad sweep of inequality in the churches of the Reformation, so now we have to look more closely at a particular doctrine that has greatly impeded progress towards the inclusiveness which equality ought to imply.

Justification by Faith

For most of the history of the Protestant churches, justification by faith alone has been the standard by which all doctrine may be judged. In the introduction, we pointed out that there was a bias towards the Pauline epistles in the preaching of Reformed ministers.

Here lies the explanation – the letter to the Romans and to a lesser extent that to the Thessalonians hammered home the importance of justification to believers and gave meaning to the ministry of Christ as not just a narrative but as the basis of the faith which alone could secure justification. *Pistis Christou*, faith in Christ, was the proof text upon which much of the documents of the Reformation were founded. The text can be found in Thessalonians 3:16 and less explicitly in places in Romans. As with the perception of a call as a sign of true acceptance by God so faith alone became a visible sign that one was saved. The articulation of the faith was seen down and throughout the hierarchy of the church from the minister preaching in the pulpit to the elder exercising discipline, right through to the father leading family prayers. The signs of faith were everywhere except in the roughest areas of society and the silent, uncomplaining private world of people with disabilities. If faith could not be taught people were forgotten. A disabled child was not present at the all-pervading Sunday school or to translate that simple gospel message into the work ethic that did not affect him or her. Justification by faith was therefore a welcome doctrine to societies looking for the liberation, which came with the new democracy of the church, and the opportunities for talented people to apply their religious insights in ways that had been denied the pre-reformation Roman church.

It would therefore seem to be the case that any move towards a broader understanding of justification would not only be welcomed by the ecumenical movement but by those who have an interest in affirming that all disabled people have an opportunity to develop a faith within an inclusive church.

In the 1980's, theologians at Yale and Princeton in the USA began to develop theories which became known as postliberal. These theories had three aims which are of interest in this context. The first was a desire to remove many of the barriers in doctrines like justification to ecumenical convergence. Second, the theories wished to show that doctrine and religious belief grows out of community belief and narrative and not from individual experience. Lastly, they wish to show that an understanding of religion could pass beyond the liberal interpretation of doctrine to a position where doctrine became the rules and the grammar by which we understand our faith which is grounded at some point in the Bible. One of the most formative books was *The Nature of Doctrine* by George Lindbeck (1984). He wrote of doctrine:

> Thus while a religion's truth claims are often of the utmost importance to it (as in the case of Christianity), it is, nevertheless, the conceptual vocabulary and the syntax or inner logic which determine the kinds of truth claims the religion can make. The cognitive aspect, while often important, is not primary.

(Lindbeck, 1984; p 35)

For the purpose of our writing these three aims come together in a critical examination of the doctrine of justification. If it could be proved that justification included all no matter what we may perceive of equality of faith, and if we could apply that to the church over all the divides of denominations, and that our approach to disabled people would be ruled by that doctrine, a way forward might be offered to the vexed question of people who have very little opportunity to articulate their faith in an otherwise articulate church.

David Harink has written on justification in his book *Paul among the Postliberals* (2003) in which he draws together work on the phrase, *pistis Christou* and the work of Karl Barth in both his commentary on Romans and volume IV of his *Church Dogmatics*. (Barth, 1956–1969) He lays the foundation of his argument by showing that many scholars have misinterpreted *pistis Christou* as faith *in* Christ when in fact it can mean the faith *of* Christ. In other words, he argues, we are justified by Christ's faith not by our own. This is how Barth consistently developed his Christology by showing that it was the agency of Christ's obedience and faith in his father that led to our justification through his righteousness. As Lewis might put it, Jesus risked complete and abject failure upon the cross, descending into Hell (a place of no hope nor of life) in the belief that his father would raise him from this death in some unknown but glorious way. (Lewis, 2001) We are justified because Jesus came through the torments of earthly pain and Hell to the glory of the Resurrection. We have an opportunity of righteousness not by the efforts of our own faith but by the undeserved faith of Jesus himself.

> God's faithfulness is revealed in the faithfulness of Jesus Christ; specifically, in the faithfulness of his standing "among sinners as a sinner," placing himself under God's judgment, and moving through slavery to the cross and to death, as Barth explicates with reference to Philippians 2:6–11.

(Harink, 2003; p 49)

If this project is finally going to work, we must insert the final condition that faith is for all and the property of all. It has been shown that the Reformation churches found plenty of reasons to discount disabled people and to consider them either without faith or with a defective faith; but here is the opportunity to adopt the first principle with the radical suggestion that community experience cannot make distinctions as an individualistic view did. The church is the new community of all; it is the community that can transcend the individualistic intellectual qualities of the few in order to include all who in any way can approach Christ in faith.

There are two ways of talking of faith in the context of God. Barth calls the act of the Resurrection the *faithfulness* of God in standing by his son and vindicating him after his humiliation on the cross. Jesus on the other hand has *faith* which is seen throughout his ministry and eventually in his kenotic act of obedience upon the cross. (Philippians 2:5–11) In that passage, which is another great hymn by Paul, Paul celebrates the fact that Jesus took on the nature of a slave and descended to depths rather than snatching at equality with God his father. In the faithfulness of both God and Jesus is the foundation of our faith. There is simply no faith without their faith first and the uniqueness of that faith is its eternal quality which cannot be surpassed. Our individual faith has no set quality in comparison and no one has the right to decide what qualities may be admired and considered acceptable in God's sight. That has always been the temptation of many in the Reformed churches and must be rejected for the possibility of every expression of faith being an equally acceptable offering to God. Every offering of faith has been determined by the nature of the cross not by the nature of our intellectual appreciation.

> The christian community is formed by the conviction that the power of this world is not the determining sway of our existence, but rather it is the power we find in the cross of Jesus Christ.

(Hauerwas in Swinton, 2004; p 154)

Equality

The word 'equality' has gained a lot of currency within disabled circles recently. It is now the chosen word to describe training. For many years, people were exposed 'disability awareness training' which showed them what it felt like to be disabled. They could be asked to use a wheelchair, wear spectacles that distorted their sight or weights and splints which made it difficult to move. This did indeed give people an impression of disability but tended to leave them with the feeling, 'thank God I am not disabled'. Such a sentiment is of limited value in the search for equality. Another attempt at training has given the life history of disabled people and pointed up their suffering and presented an apologia for the anger and militancy which they now feel. This too may have negative results because they turn the listener off and reinforce stereotypes of people with disabilities as people with grudges and grievances against society.

'Disability equality training' (DET) emphasises those actions which people may take to stress the equality of people with disabilities have with anyone else. Thus the course may try to eliminate disablist language – words which are now considered to be insulting like 'spastic', 'cripple', 'Mongol' or 'backward'. It stresses the advantages of making buildings and products accessible and shows the advantages of offering employment to disabled people. The overall message of such training is to suggest that if barriers are removed, there are true opportunities for participation in society with equal status.

In the conclusion, the question will be asked whether inclusion actually works as a policy. It is very easy of include people in the church whilst denying equality. Thus, Nancy Eisland can devote a chapter of her book, *The Disabled God*, to the failure of some American churches to accept that full inclusion of disabled people includes equality in ministry and in participation of the churches' governance. (Eisland, 1994; 75ff)

This book has stressed that equality was central to Paul's manifesto for the new church and such views of equality have carried forward in documents as diverse as St Augustine through to the American constitution. Equality has inspired many revolutions and the quest for it has toppled many governments. Whilst Paul cannot take all the credit, much has been inspired by a religion that embraces equality before God and in fellowship above all. In terms of the Reformation, the argument might run that the hierarchies of the older non-reformed churches bred corruption of both a material and spiritual kind. However, we must confine consideration to a narrower view, but possibly more important viewpoint, of equality. As one commentator on equality and the rights of man in modern society comments, '... even if a society does not need love, men, in fact, do'. (Beneton, 1993; p 12)

Christian equality is different from normal expectations of what it should be. It demands more quality and circumscribes equality among men and women by the law of Christ and the nature of our souls. Once again it has been our ability to judge people, for which we have no warrant, which has created inequalities in our community, the church, which should be equal in every aspect.

St Augustine set out the agenda in *The City of God*, when he makes every soul a potential citizen despite the obvious fact that many of us fail to qualify.

> In a certain sense Augustine was the first one-worlder. He took a highly inclusive view of what constitutes a human being:
>
> What is true for a Christian beyond the shadow of a doubt is that every real man, that is, every mortal animal that is rational, however unusual to us may be the shape of his body, or the color of his skin, or the way he walks, or the sound of his voice, and whatever the strength, portion or quality of his natural endowments, is descended from the single first-created man.
>
> (Brennan and Coons, 1999; p 259 quoting Augustine, *City of God,* 365, 367)

What Brennan and Coons are pointing out is that Augustine accepted that all men and women were uniquely created with different gifts, appearances and demeanours that have to be respected equally as citizens of the earthly and heavenly city. Such a doctrine is the embodiment of *Imago Dei* which stems from the conviction that humanity is made in the image and likeness of God. Such a doctrine has been central to the recent linking of the WCC on all aspects of humankind especially minorities such as people with disabilities. Most theories of equality deal with the fact of difference but Judaism and Christianity both demand that we take seriously the fact that God has sanctioned differences and demands our respect for them.

St Thomas Aquinas argued that it was in the law of God and of Christ that we found a commandment to love our neighbour and implied that within that love was an equality which marked the Christian community. (*Summa*, Book 3, §117) Many since have argued that equality arises out of Christian fellowship and from no other source. St Paul perhaps introduced a revolution into religious thought in that his entire model for the church assumed that everyone was universally entitled to receive the grace of Jesus Christ in faith. Preceding all other commentators, Paul offered an idealistic vision of equality within the fledgling church. Badiou, writing from a French point of view, offers an insightful vision of the equality being equal to that which is expected in French society. (Badiou, 2003) Christian equality is more intangible than the modern equality which Beneton was eager to criticize because it is spiritual and cannot be easily enshrined in a constitution, yet it challenges the members of the Christian fellowship to a greater acceptance of one another than does secular society. Aquinas was absolutely correct in suggesting that the obligations of love demanded more than some of us are able to give out of our sinful and weak nature.

Thus, the church has been challenged at various times to extend a feeling of acceptance and equality to different groups within their midst. The struggle is far from over but has moved from favouring those with obvious signs of economic and social success to groups which claim minority status and past persecution or neglect. People with disabilities are one such group and although it may be argued that the church has never deliberately withheld love from them; it is undoubtedly the case that it is not extended that love to equality. The form love took, and in which it still manifests itself, is one of charity offered in good faith but without any regard to the implications of equality. What disabled people cannot expect within the church is equality without a Christian reference. This is perhaps the problem which faces other minorities like homosexuals and the great majority of women. In both these cases, as with people with disabilities, Christian equality can only be created by careful theological investigation and an understanding of the biblical encouragements and obstacles to full integration. This is why it is important that the inclusion of disabled people within the church be tackled theologically and not just as a legalistic response to Acts of various legislatures outlawing discrimination.

Conclusion

There can be no better place to look for a summary of this chapter than to depart from St Paul and look at words from St Peter:

... you are a chosen people, a royal priesthood, a holy nation, a people belonging to God, that you may declare the praises of him who called you out of darkness into his wonderful light. (1 Peter 2:9)

Few words in the epistles can be quite as encouraging as the above verse from 1st Peter. It message is clear yet mysterious, and it sums up so much of what has been discussed about being chosen, justified or being equal in the new fellowship which is the Church. It is almost too imperialistic in tone but, in fact, should humble the true reader. We are indeed a chosen people belonging to God and called out of darkness to light, but are we 'royal'? Paul makes mention of running for a crown of glory on more than one occasion but emphasizes that it is not a crown or a glory of our making but of God's. (1 Corinthians 9:25, 2 Timothy 2:5) We have seen how it was obtained through the faithfulness of God and the faith of Jesus. Any glory belongs to them alone and we only have to think of the crown of thorns to realize that the crown is not necessarily bedecked with jewels and ermine. We are called into a priesthood of believers who share the burdens and the joys of the Christian faith in a spirit of equality and fellowship. The word priesthood reminds us that it is dependent on gifts – gifts which come with our calling and acceptance into the fellowship of Christ.

This is also comes with a recognition that these gifts are available to all. We, as lesser mortals, can always succumb to the temptation to enjoy the trappings of royalty at the expense of those who we consider less worthy of such a title. Peter warns against idle gossip by which he may mean the temptation to talk disparagingly of fellow members of the Church denying them the same inheritance which we accord to ourselves. (1 Peter 2:1) The 'royal priesthood' is for all and it is our duty to ensure that it remains so. If this chapter has been talking about inclusion, it is here that inclusion must confer gifts on all of the fellowship. People with disabilities have a right to aspire to this priesthood as anyone else and may bring a variety of gifts into the midst of the fellowship as would any other group. Their gifts may only become truly apparent when they are allowed to flourish in the midst of a fertile fellowship. Past generations have tended to place them below the pecking order of the royal priesthood, but with our growing awareness of the talents that may come forth as barriers are removed so their worth within this status can be recognized.

The next verse continues the argument:

> [10]Once you were not a people, but now you are the people of God; once you had not received mercy, but now you have received mercy. (1 Peter 2:10)

The essence of God's choice is that through the resurrection of his son Jesus a new people was born who went far beyond the limits of the Israel of old. The church is now the new Israel and into it are called Gentiles and Jews alike. The righteousness of Jesus was the justification of our righteousness; the faithfulness of Jesus the justification for our faith. God in his mercy had called us to be the new people of the new covenant. If we are unable to accept the extent of this new people to include all of God's creation, our understanding is sorely lacking. If we can accept that all are potentially called from sin into this fellowship, we are on the way to understanding inclusion and perhaps accepting its weaknesses as well.

Chapter Seven

The Nature of Inclusion

This book has been about St Paul's attitude to inclusion and has attempted to show that he sought to include many groups that had been previously excluded from full participation in matters of faith. His major project was to unite Jews and Gentiles in a common faith in Christ. However, he also offered women a new role in faith and extended the offer to slaves and other groups that that previously lacked opportunities. Disability was an issue in his personal life but would not have been a burning issue of the time. Nevertheless, this does not prevent us from drawing implications for today's reading of his epistles.

At first sight, the word inclusion is relatively simple: it is welcoming all into the worshipping church and offering them confirmation of this welcome in baptism and in the sharing of a common meal. The word 'inclusion' has more complicated meanings, and has taken on definitions, that have restricted its use by pointing out its limitations. These limitations can be summed up in the idea that people may be included in any activity but not offered equality. They can be included in worship but not offered equal rights of participation. Many churches offer excellent access but have failed to extend the access to the chancel where more of the activities of worship take place. Children have long been included in worship but have had their participation limited to the children's address or a 'family service'. Children are not capable of enjoying equality so that this restricted participation is acceptable but when we come to adults with disabilities, we must ask whether their participation demands equality.

The issue of definition is not just confined to equality. Inclusion, or an inclusive church, has become a byword in certain circles, particularly in America, for the inclusion of gays and lesbians, so much so that the *World Council of Churches* self-consciously avoids the term when dealing with disability. Any internet search will confirm that most discussions of inclusion in the church are about the acceptance of the homosexual community. The attention paid to this minority is almost as great as that paid to women in previous decades for two reasons. Firstly, both groups were, and are, very vociferous and organized. Secondly, both present the church with a doctrinal issue, which is not only interesting, but came to the fore in many a theologian's thinking. They are also issues which challenge our understanding of scripture to an extent that disabilities does not. To those who believe in the veracity of scripture, homosexuality is condemned and the place of women is greatly circumscribed by some of the utterances of Paul, and by the circumstances that made it unlikely that Jesus would include women in his ministry because of the culture of his time. To those of a liberal persuasion all the biblical references can be challenged as relative and the result is that a strong and intriguing debate can result. In calling inclusion the end result, theologians have created an aim for their debate that is not so apparent in the case of disability. Inclusion, in these debates, is defined by the goal of equal participation for groups which have little reason for not being considered equal.

The problem with the debate about including disabled people in the church is that there is no consensus about the nature of equality as governing the meaning of inclusion. It is not a doctrinal issue since no one really holds to the importance of the laws of Leviticus today and all may reasonably agree that the text in Leviticus 21:16 – 23 referred very specifically to the priestly order within the Levites and not to a general prescription which lasts to this day. Therefore, the debate is really free of doctrinal issues and really boils down to an understanding of what is to be achieved in bringing disabled people fully into the body of the church. The mistake is to make the argument purely mechanical at the expense of theology and a greater understanding of the wider meaning of inclusion.

There seems to be a propensity to write about inclusion and people with learning difficulties and, in particular, children. Simon Bass writes of the need to include children with special needs in the churches educational programmes and stresses the obligations imposed by the DDA. There are many similar groups and organisations with a concern for such disadvantaged individuals but the majority tended to deal with children. It is indeed the case that by integrating disabled children into the church, the opportunity is also offered to the parents to attend freely. There is a story of one minister who visited a family he thought he knew well. The family had three children but his records only had two because the parents never brought their disabled child to church in case his behaviour was disruptive. It may be, however, that the church feels more easily empowered to include children with disabilities than adults because all children are included on their own terms. Sunday School and family services remain a specialized form of inclusion which cannot be extended to adults with disabilities in the preface to Simon Bass's book, *Special Children Special Needs* (2003), the Bishop of Rochester reminds readers that integration must extend to all who are disabled and not just to children. The urgency behind the impetus behind the inclusion of children may be the widespread belief that they are the future of the church and that they are more easily brought to faith than adults are. Another reason may be that it is easier and less intrusive to adapt children's and worship and learning than to take the major steps required to provide full access to the participation adults with disabilities into the full life of the church. Yet another reason is that when disabled adults without learning difficulties are discussed, they have autonomy of thought that is thought to be lacking in people with learning difficulties. In fact, such adults may have as many doubts and reasons for resistance as anyone else.

This brings us to the next most important issue about inclusion. As soon as you move from children, you move into an area of respecting people's responsibilities and rights. All disabled people have these and expect them to be respected in the context of the church as with any other sphere of life. There is a huge debate about the meaning of inclusion which divides left from right, politician from politician and social worker from social worker.

Under New Labour, and similar schemes in America and other progressive countries, inclusion is sought as a way of reducing dependence upon the state and the development of lack of dependency on welfare. In America, this is the main argument in favour 'small government' – the idea that overbearing welfare creates its own dependence and stifles individual creativity. In the UK, 'social inclusion' is sought for all groups who show marked dependence upon the state. Such people include those on incapacity benefit or long-term income support, single mothers and groups of middle-aged men and women who have ceased to be able to participate in the labour market. Social inclusion is synonymous with a return to work and a reduction in dependency of benefit. It is market led and places demand not upon the state but upon the individual. This is the ultimate belief in responsibilities and could not be further from catering for children in the church context. This represents a debate with which the church is not fully engaged either in its own terms or on political terms as a pressure group.

Academics like Neil Gilbert (2002) and John Pierson (2001) rightly point out the hidden agendas of social inclusion in a political climate that demands lower taxes and less intrusive government. Pierson, however, draws attention to the policies of social inclusion which were started by the Scottish Office and continued by the Scottish Executive who have a unit dedicated to social inclusion within their civil service.

> [Social exclusion is] a shorthand label for what can happen when individuals or areas suffer from a combination of linked problems such as unemployment, poor skills, low income, poor housing, high crime environments, bad health and family breakdown. Different people will take the term to mean different things - many see it as another term for multiple deprivation, social disadvantage or poverty. Others prefer to talk about the need positively to promote social inclusion. In broad terms, however, social exclusion is taken to mean more than *material lack of income*.

(Scottish Office, 1998; p 2)

There is reason to believe that neither the Scottish Executive nor the UK Government has an aggressive desire to cut back on benefits as the real agenda of social inclusion. No. 10 has a strategic unit which has produced a report, *Improving the life chances of disabled people* (2005). This uses the concept of increasing life chances for disabled people. The strategic plan cuts across many departmental divisions and seeks to give seamless opportunities to disabled people by ensuring that benefits do not conflict, thus bringing together benefits in such a way that they do not cause a poverty trap or disincentives to resuming work or entering mainstream life. The plan also deals with education in recognising that barriers are often erected instead of enabling policies which allowed disabled people ready access to education at all stages. The key to understanding it is to recognise that it is talking, not of inclusion but of increased opportunities and the breaking down of barriers, which have been erected by government itself.

There seems, therefore, to be a distinction between a simple desire to save money on welfare by including people and easing the path into mainstream activities, which may in turn lead to a drop in dependence on welfare. Unless our government moves considerably to the right, there seems to be little evidence that inclusion is simply a device to reduce the welfare bill but social inclusion, in any guise, must also lead to social equality. Equality cannot be achieved if people are not in mainstream activities and they cannot expect to achieve equality on benefit alone, which means that social inclusion must in fact imply less dependence upon welfare. It is only when people are told that their worth is diminished by their dependence on benefits, that the inequalities become insidious and lacking the compassion of the original intentions.

It is obvious that there are many hidden meanings in inclusion and that they are not all for the benefit of the excluded. How may the church offer inclusion to disabled people in such a way that it avoids some of these hidden meanings in the term? To achieve this, we must first extract the key words from the foregoing pages. The first is 'equality'. Second is 'opportunity'. Third is 'independence';

and the last is 'compassion' although this is not stated. Actually, the word 'compassion' implies a great deal which we tend to take for granted, and should perhaps be dealt with first.

Christians have always been compassionate and have been long aware that Jesus wept out of compassion, giving us an example *par excellence*. However, Jesus' compassion was followed by action – he brought Lazarus back from the dead. Martha and Mary were looking for considerably more than kind words or religious platitudes. In the same way, there are occasions when we may want to weep at the sight of a disabled person or because of our knowledge that they are being ignored or excluded by the fellowship of the church but tears in themselves achieve nothing. Compassion turns in on itself and becomes a disabling emotion in our lives. Some of the worst features of pietism have been displayed by misplaced compassion and much of the anger and indignation, which is aimed at some of the old-fashioned language of L'Arche or of Hauerwas, has been because compassion has been well expressed but poorly dealt with. The sign of the failure of compassion is when we objectify the object of our compassion; the sign of compassion well directed is to understand the deepest feelings of the object of our compassion and to act accordingly. The body of Christ should never offer compassion unless it is going to change itself materially to accommodate its object.

The argument of the right, which was referred to several paragraphs ago, is often about the stifling nature of welfare. After someone has been on welfare for a long time, his or her dependence breeds incapacity and inhibits a desire to explore possibilities on one's own. This is a most persuasive argument and can be applied to the church. In the church, there is often a great desire to welcome and include marginalized groups, such as people with disabilities, yet often they are welcomed with a compassion which does not promote integration. I have been welcomed into many churches but have been ignored or discriminated against despite the welcome of a ramp and good access. Compassion also has the danger that people within the church do not look beyond their basic obligation towards charity to the greater task of full integration. The DDA is not a charitable charter but a road map towards full integration in the church. I believe that the church should be less compassionate and more pragmatic in their policies of welcoming strangers into their midst.

Having dealt with the last, we now move to the first – 'equality'. We need to remind ourselves that baptism offers equality to all who receive it. This was a major issue in Paul's time where Jew and Gentile were brought together by the same rite of initiation, which included slaves and women. If Paul wrote today, he would surely have realised that disability was an issue and included this in the revolutionary equality that was made available to all new Christians. If we decide to include people in our midst, we can only do so based on equality. There is no greater social end for the church and, at the Last, God's sense of equality will be far greater than ours. In practical terms, accepting people on an equal basis means that they must have no more or no less privilege than anyone else but it may well be that in order to achieve this we have to honour groups who have been traditionally neglected. Disabled people must be so honoured that their gifts are able to be revealed in such a way that equality becomes irresistible. A policy of demanding of equality, not only as part of social justice, renders it irresistible as a practical reality.

The second issue which was raised was that of opportunity. As long as disabled people are stuck in a corner behind a pillar in the least attractive part of the church or are not given the tools to follow the order of service, there can be no meaningful inclusion. The churches have made an astonishing mistake in believing that the DDA is only about access to buildings. It is about keeping current employees – ministers – in employment when they become disabled. It is about being able to offer services on an occasional basis such as weddings or funerals that can allow disabled people to take part at the front of the church on the same basis as anyone else. In addition, it is about allowing elders to continue to carry on their duties after they have been incapacitated by mobility problems that make the steps in the church a daunting prospect.

There is a sense in which 'opportunity' can be synonymous with welcoming people into their midst. Welcoming is a principle duty of a Christian fellowship but can only be so if the welcome is truly into the complete fellowship of the body.

> Creation is good but finite; good life implies its finiteness, because all life will die. It is through relationships, through life in community that what is a limitation or impairment for the individual may become a gift for others in the community. We are created for community and meant to further and enhance each other's gifts so that the God-given potential of each member of the community may be realized and thus the goodness of life be manifested. Being liberated from the oppressive thought of falling short of the goodness of human life as God intended it,

(Raiser, 2003)

There can be no true fellowship unless the opportunity is forwarded to all to partake fully in the activities and sacraments of the church. If these are denied disabled people, there is little fellowship created. Sometimes the denial comes from the disabled person him or herself but more often it is due to the inability to offer full integration to the offices of the Church and its ministry. The church is, as a WCC *Faith and Order* consultation at Louvain said in 1971, essentially a body characterized by 'conciliarity' and must not exclude any segment of humanity including people with disabilities. (Vischer, 1971; p 226ff) A church which has a 'glass ceiling', or in this context a wheelchair ceiling, is one which is not taken seriously the full nature of its fellowship and obligations to extend opportunities to all.

Last, a brief word about independence. If the church decides as it can welcome and integrate disabled people, it must ensure that people with disabilities achieve their goals independently. Concessions are misguided signs of compassion and lead to resentments amongst those who have been artificially raised to an office or whatever. Independence implies that people with disabilities are accessed on their own abilities, trusted on their own abilities and promoted on their own abilities rather than because of some compassionate conspiracy.

Saint Paul has certain groups in mind when he wrote about inclusion. They were appropriate to his time but now we can apply his principles to other groups, such as people with disabilities. By way of summary, we can examine how Paul dealt with his friend and servant Onesimus in his letter to Philemon. It is an interesting study which shows the aspects of inclusion which have been outlined in the past few paragraphs. His treatment of Onesimus is not to be regarded as an early manifesto for the abolition of slavery. Glancy makes it clear that we should not 'take this ambiguous letter as a starting point for discovering early Christian attitudes toward runaway slaves or slavery more broadly is a futile enterprise.' (Glancy, 2002; p 92) We may however understand the broad aims of Paul in his treatment of a hitherto neglected group as part of the baptized fellowship. Philemon was the head of a slave owning family who, for one reason or another, had lost Onesimus to Paul in prison and Paul was pleading for his re-acceptance into his household when Onesimus returned. He was to be treated with compassion, called a 'brother' and accorded equality within baptism and faith.

> 8 Therefore, although in Christ I could be bold and order you to do what you ought to do, 9 yet I appeal to you on the basis of love. I then, as Paul—an old man and now also a prisoner of Christ Jesus— 10 I appeal to you for my son Onesimus, who became my son while I was in chains. 11 Formerly he was useless to you, but now he has become useful both to you and to me.
>
> 12 I am sending him—who is my very heart—back to you. (Philemon 1:8–12)

It is very obvious that Onesimus was valued because he had a function in the fellowship of Paul's followers. He was serving Paul and could be useful to Philemon within the context of faith. Without offering the right of participation there is no future in inclusion. Paul regarded him as a son, in other words, he showed

Christian love towards him. Then in the verses which follow he stresses the need for equality and mutual respect within the christian faith. Despite the fact that Philemon is a slave owner, he has an obligation to respect and to show love towards those who are part of his fellowship.

> 15 Perhaps the reason he was separated from you for a little while was that you might have him back for good— 16 no longer as a slave, but better than a slave, as a dear brother. He is very dear to me but even dearer to you, both as a man and as a brother in the Lord. (Philemon 1:15–16)

These verses contain a perfect example of how any person should be received by a Christian fellowship, not as inferior but as equal in every way and as deserving of love.

If these principles are applied to the inclusion of disabled people, there can be no doubt that their welcome into the church would be one as equal participants rather than people who have to overcome the first physical barrier of access.

> What this letter does offer, however, is a remarkable model of transformation, a paradigm of what ensues when one endeavors to see another human being with eyes reconditioned by the resurrection of Jesus Christ.

(Dunham, 1998)

These words of Robert Dunham sums up the mystery behind the practical problems which Paul had to address and puts the entire letter in the context of all of Paul's epistles. To include someone is to see them in a different light and to offer them the same position you have yourself in terms of esteem and Christian function in order to bring about the transformation of and into the body of Christ.

In *The Cost of Discipleship* (1959–2001), Dietrich Bonhoeffer writes of cheap and costly grace and argues that Jesus exemplified the latter in his faithfulness even to the cross. It is possible to talk of cheap and costly inclusion which is not about money but about the amount of effort individuals and congregations put into trying to include disabled people in the Church of today. Of course, inclusion has financial implications. Access and adaptation do not come cheaply, but this is not the point.

The point is that congregations must choose between token inclusionism and the full inclusion of disabled people into the life of the Church. This is costly in that it involves changing traditions and rituals to meet the needs of those who cannot take for granted the everyday movements of the congregation and must find their own ways of partaking at the Lord's Table or understanding the intricacies of sermons or the purple prose of well composed prayer. To offer access in these matters must involve preparation and thought and will be costly in terms of one's commitment of time and energy by, for instance, distributing orders of service by email on a Friday for the following Sunday. Such an act is not expensive but it could be very costly in terms of one's discipline. No more preparing services on a Saturday night! Cheap inclusion 'parks' disabled people where they will not be noticed as spectators. Costly inclusion brings these people right into the heart of the ritual and *koinonia* of the Church. Cheap inclusion believes that the governance of the Church does not need disabled people in positions of authority; costly inclusion makes this possible at every level and far beyond the legal requirements of the DDA and employment law.

A Church which includes everyone will be a lively Church and one with great opportunities for all to develop their gifts and to offer them to the glory of God, and or the enrichment of the members of the body of Christ.

Conclusion

St Paul often contrasted the law with grace and addressed a blessing to many of those to whom he wrote in terms of the 'the grace of the Lord Jesus Christ'. This has certain parallels in the area of social inclusion that are important to this conclusion. Paul lived by grace and trusted that his followers would do likewise and he repeatedly offered advice, which reminded people that individuals like Onesimus were as full of grace as any other baptized believer. Grace is a state of equality and inclusion in the body of Christ that cannot and must not be denied anyone who enters that state.

From this understanding of grace, two conclusions may be reached that lead us to the understanding the profundity of Paul's acceptance of all who are baptized and shared the common meal which came to be known as the Eucharist.

First, the Church in the UK has recently become greatly concerned about access for disabled people. This has been kick-started and motivated by the legal requirements under the *Disability Discrimination Act (1995)*. After nine years of its existence, Part 3 came into force in October of 2004 making it illegal for churches to continue to have barriers to access without reasonable excuse. Access, thus, became a legal matter whilst the broader issue of inclusion remained a matter of gracious acceptance of people who are different into the fellowship of the church. The real issue facing the churches is to marry access and inclusion into a marriage of fruitful acceptance of people with disabilities into the heart of the fellowship.

Second, Paul expects us to find gifts of grace in all and allows very few excuses for total exclusion from the fellowship of Christ. In fact, you are more likely to exclude yourself than to be deliberately excluded but, as we have seen in previous chapters, many have been accidentally excluded by the prejudices of others.

Third, and by way of introduction, Paul spent a disproportionate number of words telling us about the 'thorn in his flesh'. Why? It could be argued that by dwelling on his own troubles, he was indulging himself either in self-pity or, as he suggests himself, boasting about his achievements in the face of adversity. John Wilkinson argues that neither is true but that rather God was using Paul's affliction for good. He argues that Paul's grace shone through his illness and offered a shining example to many of his congregations and to us. (Wilkinson, 1998; Chapter 19) This is a very controversial view because it implies that God delighted in Paul's affliction, which was surely not the case, but rather that by other people accepting that Paul carried with him an affliction his gifts were allowed to blossom within their midst. The point of real import is that Paul manifested a special kind of grace that was not simply brought forth by faith but by action in his own life in a special way that showed the richness of his life in its fullness.

Returning now to the marriage between the Church's obligation to the civil law, in the form of the DDA under UK law, and the imperative to include people with disabilities graciously, we must explore the relative weakness of the former and the strengths of the latter, i.e., grace.

Many commercial buildings and probably churches are aiming to be 'DDA compliant'. Such buildings build a ramp to one entrance, install an accessible toilet not infrequently miles from where people might want to use it, and provide places for wheelchairs in churches. To do this is to obey the letter of the law whilst ignoring all the issues which other disabled people may have. It would be very cheap and easy to provide emailed copies of the order of service to those who request it sometime before the Sunday service. If blind people know what hymns are to be sung and what readings will be used they can find them on computer and put them into a format which they find suitable prior to the service. The point is that most churches are going little further than being compliant and some are 'counting the number of angels on a pinhead' in an attempt to understand what are minimal requirements to avoid discrimination. Therefore, if no one has access to a toilet, there is no discrimination; or if orders of service are not provided, it follows that people with sight impairments are not placed at a disadvantage. Compliance is an insidious way of meeting the requirements of any law and whilst we would condemn 'tax dodgers' for finding loop holes in tax law, we are much more lax about churches compliance with the DDA. Churches are the one group in society who have an obligation to go further than compliance, not for the sentimental reason that it is the christian thing to do but because not to do so is to deny access to the fellowship of the church. People must participate in the *koinonia*.

It is a tragedy of modern Britain that our cathedrals must survive as tourists attractions rather than the live places of worship. Visitors may view the architecture in a purely passive way without any knowledge of the Christianity of centuries which is enshrined within the transcendence of the stone. Rosslyn Chapel, near Edinburgh, has become a key to the *Da Vinci Code* rather than a monument to the faithfulness of the stonemasons and Sir William St Clair and family who founded it in 1446. In a similar way, people with disabilities may be accepted into churches almost as tourists who are allowed to see the worship but not to participate at any depth or higher level than the pew. Such a tragedy is unfolding before our very eyes as more and more churches become compliant and then rest on their laurels. Disabled people must not be welcomed as tourists but as potential leaders and valued participants in the ongoing development of *koinonia* which transforms a building into a church.

In order to marry access compliance with inclusion of people with disabilities, the church must take seriously the question of participation. Of course it is glamorous to measure a church's disability policy by the number of disabled ministers it has in its employ but this is to miss completely the needs of members who wish to hold a lesser office or have talents which can offer services to the congregations of which they are members. It also fails to recognise the needs of the disabled man or woman who are denied a wedding which is all ways equal to anyone else's. Even in death, a person may be denied a eulogy by a treasured friend who is disabled because there is no access to a suitable speaking place in the church. Until churches succeed in offering access on an equal basis, there will be little less than compliance within our churches and disabled people will remain 'tourists' on the outside.

Many awards have been made for damages against firms who have flouted the DDA. Some of these damages are stated to be for 'hurt to feelings'. To have one's feelings hurt in a church is unexpected and therefore much more painful and some day someone will complain that their feelings have been hurt by their exclusion. It probably will not be a church member but someone who feels excluded from an occasional service or mortified by the language used by the presiding minister. I attended a funeral of a disabled friend in a relative small church recently. In the congregation were at least ten wheelchairs users in highly visible positions. The minister insisted on saying repeatedly 'let all stand'. Someday such thoughtless language is going to be tested in a court just as a shop assistant talking through a disabled person to their assistant may be similarly tested.

The Church has a marriage waiting to be consummated, that of its obligations to conform to the DDA and its obligations to treat people with equality which is implied in baptism as we have received it from St Paul. It is also vital when people gather around the Lord's Table expecting to share his gifts in common and in equality of faith.

Many of the chapters have shown how groups such as L'Arche have included people with learning disabilities in the church and understood the centrality of the Lord's Table as a meeting place not just as a sacrament of the church, but as an expression of everyone's basic need to eat together in society. Several authors in the past have stressed how important it is to welcome disabled people into the midst of the church. Jenni Weiss Block calls us to 'copious hosting' which implies that we must extend a welcoming hand far beyond the normal expectations of an invitation. (Block,

2002) John Swinton calls for 'solicitous caring' in much the same vein. (Swinton, 2000) Both suggest that the church must find ways of changing its patterns to make people feel at home in the midst of the strangeness of what the church considers normal. What it regards as normality is often alien to countless unchurched people in the community, let alone to those who must find a level that meets a need and abilities. In a book on AIDS, entitled *The Church with AIDS: Renewal in the Midst of Crisis*, we find the following definition of justice and righteousness: -

> The biblical meaning of righteousness is justice, or "putting things right." Those who share with God in mending the creation share in God's justice. The sacraments are about God reaching out on the cross to make things right, and about God's continuing action on behalf of groaning creation. Here we find the gift of righteousness and justice, and are called to right administration of those gifts together with others in need of God's justice.

> (Susan E. Davies, 'Oppression and Resurrection Faith' in Russell, 1990: p 140)

Inclusion is achieved through hard work. The gifts, which people have, do not reveal themselves without a struggle and that struggle is part of the unfolding of God's perfect creation. When we meet at the Lord's Table, we should do so aware of each other's strengths and weaknesses and we should perhaps reflect that often weaknesses are more visible than strengths, which must be encouraged to show themselves in the midst of the practice of the church. Some weaknesses are inherent in all of us, but we must not allow weaknesses to dictate how we feel about someone. A previous chapter wrote of how some people objectivize disabled people calling the objects of their concern weaknesses whereas they may be strengths which are of the very essence of the person's personality. Susan Davies describes this process well:

> The oppression of any group, such as women; people of color; gay men and lesbians; the poor; the physically, mentally, or emotionally disabled; or the old, begins with a defined norm of personhood. Such a norm is a standard, sometimes unspoken, that declares who

is the most real, the most fully human, the most thoroughly acceptable kind of person in any given situation. Oppression has its origins in the use of that standard to judge all people and to enforce the exclusion or punishment of those who do not meet the standard. Those outside the standards are experienced as "other" by those who fit the norm, and treated as though they were less than fully human.

('Susan E. Davies, 'Oppression and Resurrection Faith' in Russell, 1990: p 92)

It is only when we see beyond the norm that we can fully accept differences and opportunities and allow these to shine as gifts, intrinsic to the person, but also indispensable to the fellowship of Christ's body.

The church has a long way to go to prepare itself to receive disabled people in this twofold way. First, the churches must allow them to shine in their own right in the midst of others. Second, to have their gifts so released that they cast light on the whole fellowship. Each one of us has a moment of epiphany within the body of Christ. At this moment, others realize the true nature of our personalities and of the treasures which have been stored 'earthen vessels' and have suddenly been broken as truths have been realized.

The digression in the last chapter into national politics and inclusion was part of a very important warning that inclusion must not be mechanistic or automatic but must indeed come from the heart, if it is going to succeed. Repeatedly, writers and groups of people have been seen to objectivize people with disabilities and have often strayed into the temptation of describing the benefits they have gained from working with such people. This ignores the fact that people with disabilities are uniquely different like anyone else and that their gifts must emerge from the fruits of a true integration into the body of Christ. To truly integrate, is ironically to be neutral on the gifts given and received and must stress rather the embodiment of each person's uniqueness as part of the body and of the gifts which must be offered to make it work. Too often disabled people are included in the Church, but only on the periphery in groups geared to their needs such as L'Arche or meetings of Prospects which offer gatherings for people with learning disabilities in separate groups and on days other than the normal worship of the Church. Such groups have done more than most to integrate disabled people into the Church but either congregations must learn from their example *en masse* or do better on their own. It is hard to know which is worse, being given access to a Church and then ignored; or offered all the services, which specialized organisations can offer, and yet be hived off from the mainstream body.

The Churches are challenged to turn access into full acceptance and to work out ways of finding what contributions people with physical disabilities and those with learning difficulties can offer to a Church which must welcome them as normal, enthusiastic members and not as 'poor victims' who must be accepted because the law demand it. Such is a negation of all that Paul stood for. He fought against slavish adherence to old Jewish rituals and turned his back upon his strict Pharisaical background in order to ensure that Gentiles who were less acceptable could have an equal place in his fledgling Christian communities which he nurtured in his Epistles. He offered advice and instructions to these communities which showed them how to cast off the old law in favour of the new law of love and of grace. Paul has challenged each generation to bring all the marginalized who felt able to be baptized into the fellowship of the Church. In this generation, people with disabilities must be high on the list of priority groups waiting to be included.

References

Abbott, L., 1898, The Life and Letters of Paul the Apostle, Houghton Mifflin Company, Boston

Badiou, A., 2003, St Paul : The Foundation of Universalism, Stanford University Press, California

Barth, K., 1956–1969, Church dogmatics; edited by G.W. Bromiley, T.F. Torrance. Vol.4, The doctrine of reconciliation, T. & T. Clark, Edinburgh

Bass, S., 2003, Special Children Special Needs, Church House Publishing, London

Beneton, P., 1993, The Languages of the Rights of Man, First Things, 37 - November

Bérubé, M., 1996, Life as We Know It, Pantheon Books, New York

Block, J. W., 2002, Copious Hosting, Continuum, New York

Bonhoeffer, D., 1959–2001, The cost of discipleship, SCM, London

Brennan & Coons, P. M. & J. E., 1999, By Nature Equal: The Anatomy of a Western Insight, Princeton University Press, Princeton, NJ

Burgess & Galloway, R. & K., 2000, Praying for the Dawn, Wild Goose Publications, Glasgow

Carlson, R. P., 1993, The role of baptism in Paul's thought, Interpretation, 7/1/1993

Chilton, B., 2004, Rabbi Paul: An Intellectual Biography, Doubleday, Toronto

Dawkins, R., 1976, The selfish gene, Oxford University Press, Oxford

Devine, T. M., 1999, The Scottish Nation, Allen Lane, The Penguin Press, London

Doty, W. G., 1983, Letters in Primitive Christianity, Fortress Press, Philadelphia

Downing, F. G., 1998, Cynics, Paul, & the Pauline Churches, Routledge, London

Dunham, R. E., 1998, Philemon 1:1–25. (Biblical analysis), Interpretation, 4/1/1998

Eiesland, N. L., 1994, The disabled God : toward a liberatory theology of disability, Abingdon Press, Nashville.

Foley (Ed.), E, 1994, Developmental Disabilities and Sacramental Access, Liturgical Press, Collegeville

References

Fritzson, A. & Kabue, S., Interpreting Disability: A Church of All and For All, WCC, Geneva

Gilbert, N., 2002, Transformation of the Welfare State : The Silent Surrender of Public Responsibility, Oxford University Press, Oxford

Glancy, J. A., 2002, Slavery in Early Christianity, Oxford University Press, Oxford

Graham, R., 2001, John Knox : Democrat, Robert Hale, London

Guarino, T., 1996, Postmodernity and five fundamental theological issues, Theological Studies, 12/1/1996

Harink, D., 2003, Paul among the Postliberals, Brazos Press, Grand Rapids, MI

Harris, J., 2002, The Social Work Business, Routledge, London

Hartin, P. J., 1999, A Spirituality of Perfection: Faith in Action in the Letter of James, Liturgical, Collegeville

Hartin, P. J., 2003, James, Liturgical, Collegeville

Hick, J., 1977, Evil and the God of love, Macmillan, London.

Hong, E. H., 2003, Kierkegaard's Concept of Existence, Marquette University Press, Milwaukee

Horrell, D., 1997, Leadership Patterns and the Development of Ideology in Early Christianity, Sociology, Vol. 58

Hull, J. M., 2001, In the Beginning There was Darkness, SCM Press, London

James, M. R., 1924, The Apocryphal New Testament, Clarendon Press, Oxford

Jones, L. G., 2000, Crafting Communities of Forgiveness, Interpretation, 4/1/2000

Küng & Tracy, H. & D., 1989, Paradigm Change in Theology, T & T Clark, Edinburgh

Lambeth Conference, 1998, Called to be a Faithful Church in a Plural World, London

Lindbeck, G. A., 1984, The Nature of Doctrine: Religion and Theology in a Postliberal Age, Westminster Press, Philadelphia

Manson, W., 1966, The Epistle to the Hebrews, Hodder and Stoughton, London

McNeill, J. T., 1952, A History of the Cure of Souls, SCM, London

Meilaender, G., 2000, Divine summons (essay on vocation), The Christian Century, 11/1/2000

Monteith, W. G., 2005, Deconstructing Miracles : From Thoughtless Indifference to Honouring Disabled People, Covenanters' Press, Glasgow

Moo, D. J., 2000, The Letter of James, Eerdmans, Grand Rapids

Murphy-O'Connor, J., 1997, Paul: A Critical Life, Oxford University Press, Oxford

Nouwen, H. J. M., 1986, In the House of the Lord, Darton, Longman & Todd, London

O'brien, R., 2004, Voices from the Edge, Oxford University Press, New York

Olkin, R., 1999, What Psychotherapists Should Know About Disability, Guildford Press, New York

Pierson, J., 2001, Tackling Social Exclusion, Routledge, London

Pilch, J. J., 1995, The Cultural World of Jesus, Liturgical Press, Collegeville, Min.

Pilch, J. J., 2000, Healing in the New Testament, Fortress Press, Minneapolis

Potter, D. C., 2001, Through Changing Scenes, Paternoster Press, Carlisle

Robinson, J. A. T., 1951, The Body, SCM Press, London

Russell, J., 1968, God's Lost Cause, SCM Press, London

Russell, L. M., 1990, The Church with AIDS: Renewal in the Midst of Crisis, John Knox Press, Louisville

Salevao, I., 2002, Legitimation in the Letter to the Hebrews, Continuum, New York

Scottish Office, 1998, Policy for Promoting Social Inclusion, Scottish Office, Edinburgh

Segal, A. F., 1990, Paul the Convert, Yale University Press, New Haven

Shuman, J. J., 2003, The Body of Compassion, Wipf and Stock, Eugene, Or.

Strategy Unit, 2004, Improving the Life Chances of Disabled People, Cabinet Office, London

Swinton, J., 2000, Resurrecting the Person, Abingdon Press, Nashville

Swinton, J., 2001, Spirituality and Mental Health Care, Jessica Kingsley, London

Swinton, J., 2004, Critical Reflections on Stanley Hauerwas' Theology of Disability, Haworth Pastoral Press, Binghampton

References

Thomas, T. K., 2000, Melchizedek, King and Priest, The Ecumenical Review, 7/1/2000

Thompson, J., 1967, The Lonely Labyrinth: Kierkegaard's Pseudonymous Works, Southern Illinois University Press, Carbondale, IL

Vanier, J., 1988, The Broken Body, DLT, London

Warrington, K., 2000, Jesus the Healer, Paternoster Press, Carlisle

Weber, M., 1958, The Protestant Ethic and the Spirit of Capitalism, Charles Scribner's Sons, New York

Wilkinson, J. J., 1998, The Bible and Healing, Handsel Press, Edinburgh

Wilson, A. N., 1992, Jesus, T. & T. Clark, London

WHO, 1980, International Classification of Impairments, Disabilities, and Handicaps, WHO Papers, Geneva

WHO, 2001, International Classification of Functioning, Disability: International Classification of Functioning, Disability and Health, WHO Papers, Geneva

Wright, N. T., 1991, The climax of the covenant : Christ and the law in Pauline theology, T. & T. Clark, Edinburgh

Yoder, J. H., 1992, Body Politics, Herald Press, Nashville

Young, F., 1990, Face to Face, T. & T. Clark, Edinburgh

Young, F., 1997, Encounter with Mystery, Darton, Longman & Todd, London

Lightning Source UK Ltd.
Milton Keynes UK
15 September 2010

159916UK00002B/29/P

9 781907 652691